incommunicado
P R E S S

D.A.P.
DISTRIBUTED ART PUBLISHERS

SELF IMAGES:100 WOMEN

A Project by Andre Rival
Edition Stemmle
Hardcover $49.95

DESIRE BY NUMBERS

Nan Golden
& Klaus Kertess
Artspace Books $15.00

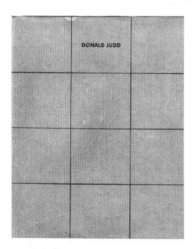

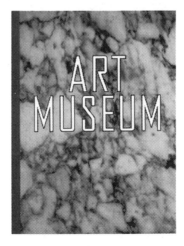

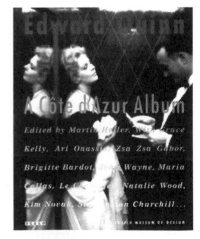

DONALD JUDD: FURNITURE

Brigette Huck,
Donald Judd
Paperbound
Museum Boymans $29.95

ART MUSEUM

Trudy Wilner Stack
Center for Creative
Photography
Paperbound $16.95

A COTE D' AZUR ALBUM

Edward Quinn
Scalo
Hardcover $16.95

 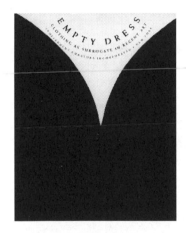 

GRAND STREET

Fetishes

53

Front cover: Yayoi Kusama, *Dressing Table*, 1990.
Back cover: Aura Rosenberg, *Women Opposite Santis, Switzerland*, 1993.

Grand Street (ISSN 0734-5496; ISBN 1-885490-04-6) is published quarterly by
Grand Street Press (a project of the New York Foundation for the Arts, Inc., a
not-for-profit corporation), 131 Varick Street, Room 906, New York, NY 10013.
Contributions and gifts to Grand Street Press are tax-deductible to the extent
allowed by law. This publication is made possible, in part, by a grant from the
National Endowment for the Arts.

Second-class postage paid at New York, NY and additional mailing offices.
Postmaster: Please send address changes to Grand Street Subscription Service,
Dept. GRS, P.O. Box 3000, Denville, NJ 07834. Subscriptions are $40 a year (four
issues). Foreign subscriptions (including Canada) are $55 a year, payable in U.S.
funds. Single-copy price is $12.95 ($15 in Canada). For subscription inquiries,
please call (800) 807-6548.

Grand Street is printed by the Studley Press in Dalton, MA. It is distributed to the
trade by D.A.P./Distributed Art Publishers, 636 Broadway, 12th floor, New York,
NY 10012, Tel: (212) 473-5119, Fax: (212) 673-2887, and to newsstands only
by B. DeBoer, Inc., 113 E. Centre Street, Nutley, NJ 07110 and Fine Print
Distributors, 6448 Highway 290 E., Austin, TX 78723. *Grand Street* is distributed
in Australia and New Zealand by Peribo Pty, Ltd., 58 Beaumont Road, Mount
Kuring-Gai, NSW 2080, Tel: (2) 457-0011.

GRAND STREET

Editor
Jean Stein

Managing Editor	*Art Editor*
Deborah Treisman	Walter Hopps
Assistant Editor	*Designer*
Howard Halle	Jim Hinchee
Editorial Assistant	*Administrative Assistant*
Julie A. Tate	Lisa Brodus

Interns
Elisa Frohlich
John Henderson
Jeffrey Rotter

Consulting Editor (Fetishes)
William T. Vollmann

Contributing Editors
Hilton Als, Dominique Bourgois, Colin de Land, Anne Doran,
Morgan Entrekin, Gary Fisketjon, Raymond Foye, Jonathan Galassi,
Stephen Graham, Barbara Heizer, Dennis Hopper, Hudson,
Andrew Kopkind (1935–1994), David Kornacker, Jane Kramer,
Erik Rieselbach, Edward W. Said, Robert Scheer, Elisabeth Sifton,
Jeremy Treglown, Katrina vanden Heuvel,
Gillian Walker, Drenka Willen

Publishers
Jean Stein & Torsten Wiesel

CONTENTS

The Duke of Dirt

I've been called the "King of Sleaze," the "Pope of Trash," the "Prince of Puke," the "Duke of Dirt," the "Ambassador of Anguish," and the "Anal Anarchist." All are fine by me, but I think the "Pope of Trash" sounds most dignified.

John Waters

HILTON ALS: I was just in bed with you for three days.

JOHN WATERS: Really?

HA: I was watching your films on video cassette.

JW: I'm glad that my films are available on video, because that way they make it to small towns. You know, if you have only one last picture show in your town, it ain't playing *Multiple Maniacs*. But I hate television. I never look at it, ever, ever, ever. Bad television to me is just bad. It's not so bad it's good. It's like having somebody in my house I don't want. I hate the light of it. I hate the crackling noise. It's good for only two things: pornography and war. What really makes me insane is when people walk into my house and turn on the TV. Relationships have ended because of television.

HA: You've broken up with people over TV?

JW: No, but I've made them wear earphones.

HA: Wow!

JW: I don't mind being on it, but I never watch it when I am.

HA: But you're amazing on film.

JW: Do you like listening to your own voice on a tape recorder? It's the same thing.

HA: Well, you were really funny in *Hairspray*.

JW: I hated being in my own movie. I'll never do that again. I don't mind being in other people's, but I hate being in my own.

HA: Why did you do it?

JW: The producers and distributors all pressured me to. Since I had never done it before, I thought, "Well, okay." And then I realized in the middle of it that I had to put on some stupid outfit and makeup and stuff.

HA: What was the inspiration for making films?

JW: Actually the first thing I ever did was to write a story at summer camp. I said, "I'm going to write a story that's going to horrify all the other campers," and the campers all said, "No, you won't." I wrote it all summer, and I read it at the last campfire. Then the camp called my parents. Because, you know, all the campers in the story were, like, slaughtered and tortured and stuff. One of the first of many phone calls from an authority figure that my parents received.

HA: How did Baltimore influence your aesthetic?

JW: Baltimore has a kind of nasty sense of humor. The people there aren't impressed by trendiness or anything. There aren't any gossip columns to be in. There's none of that stuff. So I got my sensibility from the movies.

I went to the drive-in every night. I went to see nudist camp movies. I was obsessed by all the lowest kinds of movies. And I would see all the art movies in New York. Then I just sort of put them together. That was what we did: we took speed and went to the movies. We'd see five a day sometimes.

HA: Did you have a coterie of friends at the time?

JW: Well, a lot of those people died, you know? It's depressing to realize how many of them did. The first generation of people I made movies with.

HA: I was looking at *Female Trouble* . . .

JW: Practically everyone from that movie is dead. I don't look at those movies now.

HA: Never?

JW: The only time I ever have to look at them is when I'm at a university giving a lecture and they're showing one. I'm trapped there, what am I going to do? The only way I actually like to watch them is in foreign languages. With subtitles.

HA: Tell me about the beginning of all this for you.

JW: I made my first movie when I was sixteen. That may be why I'm not dead, because I always knew what I wanted to do.

HA: In Baltimore?

JW: Yeah. But I used to run away to New York all the time and go to the Gate Theater and the Bridge Theater and see all the underground movies. I went to the world premiere of *The Chelsea Girls*.

HA: Did you lose your mind?

JW: I wanted to lose it, let's put it that way. I recently went to see *Beauty #2* and *Poor Little Rich Girl* again, nearly thirty years later. A friend said,

"Thank God the superstars were on speed. Imagine what they would've been like normally." Because their conversation wasn't even witty or interesting or anything. It was torture to listen to. So I liked it a lot, actually.

HA: So, the first film at sixteen . . .

JW: The first film at sixteen was *Hag in a Black Leather Jacket.* It was filmed on the roof of my parents' house: a white man and a black man being married by a Ku Klux Klan guy. In my mother's wedding dress. I was in high school then. Then I went to N.Y.U. and got thrown out of there for pot in the first drugs-on-campus bust.

JOHN WATERS' *Desperate Living* Starring LIZ RENAY • MINK STOLE • SUSAN LOWE • EDITH MASSEY • MARY VIVIAN PEARCE • and introducing JEAN HILL Produced and Directed by JOHN WATERS From NEW LINE CINEMA

HA: Were you at N.Y.U. for film?

JW: Yeah, I guess. I only went to one class. I wonder what I was eventually going to tell my parents when my report card came. They would call and say, "How's school?" I'd say, "Fine."

HA: What were you doing?

JW: Getting high and going to movies. But I wonder, if I hadn't been thrown out, what I would have eventually told them when I got zero in every subject. "Oh, it was a hard test." I don't know. I didn't think that far ahead. Which is amazing to me, when I look back on it.

HA: You seem like a very precise person now.

JW: I guess my father's personality seeped through all the lunacy.

HA: What was your first big-budget film?

JW: I haven't made it yet. I mean *Serial Mom* was $13 million, and that's half the cost of a real Hollywood movie. *Polyester* was really the first that was filmed in 35 mm, and it cost $300,000 in 1981. That felt like a huge budget then.

HA: What kind of fetishes do you use in your movies?

JW: I always use sexual fetishes because they look so ridiculous. "Shrimping"—toe-sucking—has been in a lot of my films because it looks so absurd. And I see these porno videos they have out that feature tickling. I really don't get how that could be erotic. Then there's the "Diaper Pail Fraternity"—grown men who eroticize wearing diapers. Did you know you can buy a bouncy chair for a 250-pound man? Now when I see "Baby on Board" signs, I think of men jerking off in carseats. I was telling a friend about it and he said, "I've been home with a baby." That's what they call each other, it's the code word. I said, "What did you do?" "I diapered him." I said, "You did? I would run right out of the house." I mean if someone said to me, "Would you diaper me?" I would be really turned off. I was shocked.

Another fetish is "Sploshing"—the erotic act of dumping food in your loved one's crotch. There are whole magazines about it that show dressed-for-success women—you know those horrible suits that women lawyers wear—sitting on pies. Does sitting on a pie work? I'm not ruining an outfit to try it out, but it is fascinating to see these people who are so serious about it. I'm thrilled that I can still be surprised by people's behavior.

HA: One of the things I've noticed in your films is that there's a lot of talk about hair. Do you have a hair fetish?

JW: Well, let's get one thing straight, if it's in my movie, it doesn't mean that I have that fetish in my personal life. As I've said many times, Hitchcock didn't kill people in the shower.

Maybe I have very thin, bad hair, maybe that's why. There's a local word in Baltimore, a hair-hopper, which means someone who spends too much time on his or her hair, and is dead serious about it. Hair-hoppers were the enemy growing up, you know, in the hippie years, but my movies have a lot of hair-hoppers in them.

Baltimore is the hairdo capital of the world. Teased hair just ended there, basically. And they have Farrah Fawcett hairdos still. She's a saint in Baltimore. I mean they could build a statue of that hairdo. The woman in my supermarket has a perfect one right now—dyed bright yellow.

My parents are sort of like George and Barbara Bush—and they wouldn't be mad if I said that. They say it themselves. My mother doesn't have a beehive and never would have. In Baltimore, there were many woman that did and I was raised to look down on them, so I looked up instead. Those big hairdos were the norm at the time. You'd see women in the laundromat with no makeup, a housedress, bedroom slippers, and a hairdo that'd be appropriate for the Presidential Inauguration. They still look like that.

HA: Why do you stay in Baltimore?

JW: Because that's what I make movies about. I don't make movies about New York art openings. I live there because that's where real people live. I can observe their behavior. It's where all my real friends are, people who've known me for thirty years, who don't ask me about the grosses. I have a nice house there. But it's not like I'm there fifty-two weeks a year. That would make me crazy, too, to be honest.

HA: Do you think of yourself as a regional director?

JW: Yes. In the best sense of the word. I guess you could say Fellini was a regional director. I have found a certain culture that I know very well that I can satirize. New Yorkers are always shocked when they come to Baltimore. They say, "Your films are not exaggerations, they're more like documentaries."

HA: One of the things in *Hairspray* that absolutely blew my mind was the way you dealt with the race issue.

JW: The Buddy Deane Show was what *Hairspray* was really about. It was the local version of the Dick Clark Show. You got famous on that show exactly like in *Hairspray*. And there were stars on the show, big stars. They were like the local Mouseketeers.... I'm going to a big reunion of it next week. Buddy's coming back and there'll be fifty- or sixty-year-old women doing the Watusi and the Locomotion perfectly. Two hundred grandmothers. It's almost a cult.

I gave that show a happy ending in the movie, but in real life it went off the air because they wouldn't let black people on. It wasn't so much Buddy, or the television station, it was the white kids' parents who said, "You aren't dancing with those . . ." It was racially tense. Baltimore was racially tense. The swimming clubs I went to were racially tense. And I went through a whole period of my life that was almost racist in reverse, where I only hung around with black people.

HA: Did your parents flip out?

JW: Well, my parents never in my life said racist stuff. They would never. They don't have any black friends, but they're way too educated and learned and polite to ever say anything racist. But there were many people who did say racist things. When I went to a public high school in seventh and eighth grade, there was only one black kid, and he was great, we hung out together.

The beatnik years were really good, because integration was very much a part of being a beatnik. You had to have integrated couples and yell out, "All right!" for no apparent reason when they played jazz. But I got beat up at the art school for having a black girl as a date. Then there was Peaches, who was a black drag queen and sang for all the straight white frat boys. They would applaud Peaches on stage and they'd dance. Then when he'd come off, they'd beat him up. It was so odd. Baltimore is the South in a way. There are whole neighborhoods in Baltimore where they say "nigger," and they don't think they're racist.

HA: So, all the people that you were attracted to . . .

JW: Attracted to?

HA: I don't mean sexually . . .

JW: It was a friendship with a whole bunch of people. It was gay and straight, black and white, everybody hanging out. The black parents were equally uptight, because they knew that when we got busted, the white kids got out and the black kids didn't.

HA: Why would you get busted?

JW: Drinking. One time we were stopped by a black cop, and he said, "You know, you can't just be like this, this isn't Greenwich Village." Even the black cop was offended to see whites and blacks together. And girls and boys. Half the guys were gay, but the cops didn't know that. They thought that with boys and girls together something sexually weird had to be going on.

HA: In *Hairspray*, Ricki Lake has one of the greatest lines in all movie history: "Oh, Link, our skin is white, but our souls are black."

JW: You see, that scene is totally from my youth, because Lutherville, Maryland, where I grew up—about thirty miles north of Baltimore—was most certainly a white neighborhood, but two blocks of it were black, and still are. And when I was a kid, I used to lie in bed and hear the blacks walking home singing a cappella Jerry Butler songs late at night. I'd lie there in bed and think it was the most beautiful thing. When I was eight years old, I knew all the good music.

HA: How did you first hear it? Just on the radio?

JW: Yeah, there were three radio stations: WSID, WEBB, and WWIN. There was Hot Rod, Fat Daddy, and Rockin' Robin. I listened to them every day and I'd go buy all the music. All the white kids did, before the Beatles. I hated the Beatles. They ruined rock 'n' roll for me. They put girl groups out of business overnight, the same way that Andy Warhol put the Abstract Expressionists out of business with his soup cans.

HA: There was a lot of strange social history going on when you were making these movies.

JW: We parodied Charles Manson—in *Multiple Maniacs*—way before anybody else did. The same way we did the Kennedy assassination two years after it happened, with Divine as Jackie in her outfit crawling all over the trunk of the car. People are offended today, but in 1966 they were *really* offended.

HA: Did they freak out at screenings?

JW: People freaked out when they saw it being filmed. The neighbors would look out in suburban Baltimore on Sunday morning, and there would go the cavalcade down the street, you know, with Divine screaming, climbing over the trunk of the car in a pillbox hat with blood all over him. My parents, God bless their souls, were pretty liberal. They'd just say, "Uh, okay." At the time, I didn't think they were being so liberal by allowing it. I just thought of course they would allow it. But now when I look back, I'm like, well, I wonder what the neighbors thought?

HA: Were your parents financing the films for you?

JW: Yeah. And I paid them back, too. Each time. And then eventually I'd ask my father for twice as much. Finally, after *Pink Flamingos* came out in '72, he said, "Okay, don't pay me back. But don't ask anymore, you're set up in business."

Those early movies, believe me, he never saw them either. They were against everything he believed in. To this day neither of my parents has ever seen *Pink Flamingos*. Why make them see it now? They've read about it.

HA: What was the reaction to your movies in the press?

JW: Really bad. There was only one critic, Lou Cedrone of the Baltimore *Evening Sun*, who always rose to the bait and gave the best kind of bad reviews that really helped us then: "This is his first sickie . . ." or "Is this part of the 'new world' they have in mind?"—which I loved. And the one we always used to quote in ads was Rex Reed: "Where do these people come from? Where do they go when the sun goes down?" We certainly had no support. But there was an audience in Baltimore and it grew each time.

HA: Tell me about meeting Divine.

JW: He was just my friend. I knew him in high school.

HA: What was his name?

JW: Harris Glenn Milstead. And I met him through a girl who lived on my street—whom I met because she had a bleached-blonde beehive that had turned green from the chlorine in swimming pools. I used to see her mowing the lawn in short-shorts with a green beehive, and I thought, "Oh, *who*'s she?" She knew Divine because they lived across the street from each other and they gambled for pimple medicine. All girls used to wear pimple medicine on their lips then.

HA: To make them white?

JW: Yeah. Like Clearasil, that was Divine's favorite makeup tone. I mean, in high school, he was almost a nerd. He never went out until he was sixteen years old. Never left his house, ever. He did his mother's hair every day and got beat up in school. Really hideously. They'd wait for him outside. The police had to take him home sometimes.

HA: They beat him up because he was so sensitive?

JW: I don't know why. He wasn't flamboyant. He was feminine, but . . . they looked deep into his soul and saw something that scared them or something. I gave Divine an outlet for all this rage that he had from school. He was never a hippie during all those years. He hated that shit.

HA: That's what he says in *Female Trouble*: "Oh, you disgusting hippie creeps."

JW: That was me, speaking through Divine, because I never liked hippies. We were yippies really, even though we didn't use that word. We were never *peace and love*, certainly. We were more like punk before it happened. Divine had rage. And he was a criminal, in a way, but a lovely one. He lived his whole life, to the day he died, beyond his means, like he was a rich movie star. And he never was. Rich, I mean.

When he moved to downtown Baltimore, he would always get into trouble with those expensive parties that he'd have in rented halls. We'd go to them, and the doorman would say, "Oh, are you here for Mr. Johnson?" or some other fake name Divine was using to dodge the bills. We'd say, "Oh, I guess." And we'd go in, and there would be these huge catered things, Divine would be in drag, and the help would steal all the liquor and run. And then the parties would last for a week.

It was pretty insane in those times. And we took a lot of LSD. The drag queens hated Divine—he made fun of them, you know, because they were square. Mostly they still are, outside of Tompkins Square. They want to be like Miss America. They're like bourgeois beauty queens, right?

But Divine was still living at home when we made those early movies.

HA: His mother didn't see him . . .

JW: His parents found his Jackie Kennedy outfit later. They didn't know he made movies or anything. They said, "What the hell is this?" And he said, "I am Jackie Kennedy." They didn't know what to say. But they used to get bills. You know, they would get bills for all his new outfits. Then Divine started going to the mailbox first to tear up the bills before they got them, so they would never know that they were deeply in debt until they would try to charge something, and the store would cut up their credit cards. Divine was pretty crazy in that way. He lived grandly always, even in the hippie years, even when we all had no money. He always smoked pot a lot and we used to trip with a very wide group of people—beatniks, straight boys, rich girls, lunatics, bank robbers. It was never a straight crowd or a gay crowd; it was totally mixed. For some reason, when we tripped, Divine would put on that album *Born Free*. And after it had played, he'd come out with a filthy old sheet wrapped around him, a towel around his head, and the shower rings for earrings, and do Dionne Warwick's greatest hits album, while the really strong acid was coming on. That was normal for us.

HA: How did he get the name Divine?

JW: I gave it to him in the bedroom of my parents' house, when we filmed this really early movie. People think it was from Genet, but if it was, I don't remember, even though I loved Genet. It probably was. But I remember it more from Catholic school, where they used that word so much.

HA: He was your great star.

JW: Yeah, he was. And he was because he was the ultimate outsider in every way: he was fat, he was a drag queen, and he didn't fit into any group. He was a fat person who dressed sexily. You know, it was never revealed in my movies that he was a man. That was never the plot. That's why *Hairspray* is still a big seller for children's birthday parties. They tell me that all over the country at every video store. I get letters ... Little girls run up to me and say, "You were in *Hairspray*." They don't know I made it. They just know I was the psychiatrist in it. They don't even know Divine was a man.

HA: Were there any other influences on your work?

JW: Bergman, and all those foreign films, because they were serious. And they had all the subject matter that was forbidden then, you know, suicide, despair, and all that kind of stuff. Fellini was a huge influence. And *8 ½* was certainly an influence on the characters I created for both Edith and Divine.

HA: Tell me about Edith Massey.

JW: I met her in this place called Pete's Hotel, where she was a barmaid— where she tends bar in my movie *Multiple Maniacs*. And she was just like that. I mean, we used to call her a Chatty Cathy doll, you know? She was from the school of hard knocks, but she was a kind, kind woman, who would never hurt anybody. I put her in this movie and I saw that audiences really liked her. Divine hated filming with her because she would take, like, thirty takes to say one thing. You know, it was hard for other actors to do scenes with her.

HA: And was Cookie from Baltimore?

JW: Oh yeah. We all met Cookie in 1969 at the world premiere of *Mondo Trasho* in a church hall in Baltimore. She had just been released from a mental institution. She won the door prize, which was dinner for two at the Little Tavern, the worst restaurant in the whole city. And we picked her up in a limousine and took her there. That's how I met her. She was a hard Janis Joplin type at the time. She's the only girl I ever knew who later had a girlfriend for eight years and still said she was straight. Basically she was.

HA: And Jean Hill, is she dead too?

JW: No, she's alive. She was at my Christmas party last year with two hospital attendants and an oxygen tank the same color as her dress. Other people were getting high on hits from her oxygen and smoking cigarettes around her. I thought she was going to explode in my living room.

HA: It seems that everyone in your movies had this completely over-developed sense of imagination.

JW: You know, doing those early films was a group effort, almost like terrorism. We knew that when they came out, people would be horrified by them. So it was like a group act of defiant behavior. I think that made everybody feel good actually. *Controlled* group madness.

Notebook Entries

Araki Yasusada was born in 1907 in the city of Kyoto, where he lived until 1921, when his family moved to Hiroshima. In 1930, he married his wife, Nomura, with whom he had two daughters and a son. In 1936, he was conscripted into the Japanese Imperial Army and worked as a clerk in the Hiroshima division of the Military Postal Service. His wife and youngest daughter died instantly in the atomic blast on August 6, 1945. His other daughter died three years later of radiation poisoning. His son, only nine months old at the time, was with relatives outside the city. Although Yasusada was active in avant-garde groups such as Ogiwara Seisensui's Layered Clouds and the experimental renga circle Oars, his work, along with that of his collaborators, Akutagawa Fusei and Ozaki Kusatao, is virtually unknown. Yasusada died in 1972 after a long struggle with cancer. In 1980, eight years after his death, his son discovered fourteen spiral notebooks filled with poems, drafts, English class assignments, diary entries, recordings of zen dokusan encounters, letter drafts, and other fragments. The selections that follow are part of a much larger collection that is currently being edited and translated.

Untitled
August 12, 1964

The sake shop hisses with its pleasures, all boiled up.

Here the young are speaking of virility and all the hidden forms.

Language on the window is backwards here, and inside the glass the small cries or clicks of things might be taken as the spirits of the flowers, in the Garden of the Ungathered . . .

There is the blur of the child, dropping from the tree.

Here is a black-haired man with a black-haired man.

There are the two sticks and a cup in Spring.

Here is a sake-burned mouth and the account of the lost cranes.

Here is a young bride's half-turned face, which is turning, as it must, to be turned towards me.

From the Diary of Rita Hayworth*

Dear Diary,

Diaries are things written by men, I am told. Nevertheless I am writing one, to see what a woman can do. What an incredible ~~day~~ night and day it ~~was~~ has been today! Clark called at 10 just as Teofilo (he still can't get the macaroni *al dente!*) brought breakfast and ~~it~~ my heart soared beyond the clouds. *We offered up prayers for a calm and peaceful voyage—"all the way to Izumi Province." Fujiwara no Tokizane arranged a farewell celebration "for the road" (not very appropriate for a ship, perhaps) at which everyone, from master to servant, became disgustingly drunk.* Why is it that only a few moments can turn ~~the darkness~~ the darkness that has ~~followed~~ enshrouded my soul into the very brightful *[sic]* day? *As the full moon grew faint in the morning sky, the provincial overseer of religion arrived to give us a farewell blessing. Everyone, high and low, old and young, was fuddled with drink. Even people who have never learned to write the figure one were merrily dancing figures of eight.*

Does he desire me in a true way? Oh, I know ~~his the stories about~~ it might not be so, and probably it is only a passing fancy on his parts *[sic].* Still, it is possible to dream, and the dreaming does do me good. Oh, Clark (sigh). Oh *I will never forget your countenance as we passed the pine-covered beaches of Uta. Pines beyond number! How many tens of centuries have they stood there? Waves wash the roots of each tree, and from each topmost branch a crane soars into the air.*

Speaking of dreaming, dear diary, I dreamed last night of ~~falling~~ being painted like a ~~cartoon~~ whore onto metal and falling for a long way through ~~the~~ some far-off air. I was crouching ~~like a cat or~~ like a toad, and my nipples were hard and ~~long~~ large as ~~thumbs~~ peppers!!!

---

*This undated piece was folded and inserted into a copy of Yasunari Kawabata's *Snow Country*. According to *The Story of English*, a crude likeness of a pinup photograph of Rita Hayworth was painted onto "Little Boy," the device dropped on Hiroshima. How Yasusada knew of this fact, and of Hayworth's butler Teofilo Zingarello, is not known. The italicized insertions come from the *Tosa Diary* (c. 936) which describes the return of a governor of Tosa province (the modern Kochi Prefecture on Shikoku Island) to Kyoto. While the diary is presented as that of one of the ladies in the party, scholars generally agree that the author was the governor himself, the legendary poet Ki no Tsurayuki.

~~That~~ This was how I had been painted by the hand of I never will know who. I felt as if I were ~~not my body~~ emprisoned *[sic]* within a body that was not my own but was, in the end, my ~~own already~~ finally true body. (I must relate this tomorrow to his Holiness Swami Ravadanada.) *The mountains and sea grow dark. Soon it becomes impossible to distinguish east from west.*

And then I woke up. Oh diary, there are times when I feel that my facilities are just going wild with haywires! *[sic]* ~~The script from Houston is~~ And I just can't seem to get myself to ~~pick up~~ study that ghastly script about ghosts. I'm such a procrastinator. ~~I wish think sometimes I could just die!~~ Having no excellence within myself, I have passed my days trying to make special impressions on everyone. Especially the fact that I have no man who will look out for my future makes me actually feel sick to ~~my stomach~~ myself! *[sic]* I don't want to bury myself in dreariness, but in the end, the courtesan on this Japanese screen seems more real than me. I imagine I ~~join~~ become her sometimes, and on moonlit nights in autumn, when I am hopelessly sad, I often go out on the balcony and gaze dreamily at the moon. It makes me think of days gone by. Teofilo says that it is dangerous to look at the moon in solitude, but something impels me, and sitting a little withdrawn I muse there. In the wind-cooled evening I play on my mouth-harp, though others probably wouldn't care to hear it. I feel that my playing betrays my sorrow, which with the music becomes ever more intense, and I become disgusted at myself—so worthless and pathetic am I!

I feel my pulse when the heart-skip strikes. And when I lift my arms to examine my breasts, I just can't help ~~count the~~ but count the pimples under my arms. Who invented shaving, anyway? Nine on the left, five on the right. And today, dear diary, I have an important announcement to make: I have resolved that on my birthday, nine months from today, I will give up alcohol forever, ~~and~~ only drinking champagne, wine or ~~sherry~~ sherry on the most special of occasions, and never, never under any circumstances, when I am alone. *From now on we row farther and farther out to sea. It is for this reason that all of these people have gathered here to see us off. Little by little, at every stroke of the oars, the watchers standing by the shore slip away into the distance, just as we on the boats, too, grow more and more indistinct to them. On the shore, perhaps, there are things they would like to say to us. On the boats there are things we would like to convey to them—but to no avail.*

~~Well~~ Well, I am sleepy now. Will Clark call again tomorrow? Life is so full of surprises, and tomorrow when I awake and the morning sun and the bluebirds ease through the gauze of my dreams, it ~~will~~ shall be the first day of the rest of my life! ~~And yet And yet~~ *As we reach the house and pass through the gate, everything stands out brightly under the clear moon. Things are even worse than we feared—there is a wilderness of decay and desolation. It looks as if, in a moment's passing, a thousand years of suffering have left their mark here. . . . There are many things which we cannot forget, and which give us pain, but I cannot write them all down. Whatever they may be, let us say no more.* Dear diary, I bid you good night!

Silk Tree Renga*

Happening to notice the willow leaves in the garden, a braille page of words

The voices of the sorority girls sing of fucking in a plaintive way

Dressing their frail bodies in armor are the young widows of the prefecture of

It was there we saw the trace ruins of an ancient dog-shooting range

So running after me was the young child whose name is Manifold

---

* By Yasusada, Ozaki Kusatao, and Akutagawa Fusei. Kusatao, the only member of his immediate family to survive the bombing of Hiroshima, was a member, with Yasusada and Fusei, of the Layered Clouds and Oars literary groups. He moved to Osaka in the 1960s. Fusei suffered, like Yasusada, from prolonged illness due to radiation poisoning and he died in 1971. He was an apprentice in a cloisonné jewelry business before the bombing.

A *renga* traditionally involves semantically or tonally linked stanzas of determined syllabic length composed in turns by two or more poets. By the nineteenth century, the form had become rigidly conventionalized and had lost the vitality given to it by masters like Sogi and Basho. It was in response to this ossification of the form that Yasusada, Kusatao, and Fusei collaborated on a large number of experimental renga between the late '30s and early '70s.

A screen of moonflowers and creeping gourds, with a thicket of cockscomb and goosefoot, evoking cocks and cunts

She told me then that the master of the house had left for a certain location in town and that I had better look for him there pronto, if I desired to speak to him

Everybody was fucking overjoyed to see him, as if he had returned from the dead

Terrified by these words he walked straight into the province of Kaga

How Ungo's sitting rock is still there after all these years

Where patches of lichen have flowered over glyphs

On the third day he drew a figure, and inside of it a detailed map of the pampas moor of Mano

Was it male or female? he loved to make them guess whether the stroke in that place was a cock or cunt

More and more he became obsessed with the seedling form of this great pine in the time of ancient gods

Thus during sitting, he had felt the Milky Way as a pair of thongs between the toes

There were countless boats, large and small, anchored in the deep harbor

He dreams of a gigantic mountain, shaped like the word which names it

There are manifold trees and plants which rise from it, saplings and great trees and plants beyond words or morphemes

Why don't you go fuck yourself, she said, throwing the thong at his head and missing

I was reminded then of the priest Noin, who had wept to find on his return visit the same tree cut and thrown into the Natori River as bridge piles by the new governor of the prefecture of

So nothing there was moistened with meaning

In fact, in the very gesture of the geisha was the retreat of a whole genre

So that Mount Chokai was made invisible on the watery beach of Shiogoshi

Or turned upon the sand into the shape of a flowering silk tree

Thus the interiors of two sacred structures of whose marvels I had heard with unbelieving ears were revealed to me

Translated from the Japanese by Tosa Motokiyu,
Ojiu Norinaga, and Okura Kyojin

YAYOI KUSAMA

Fortress of
Shooting Stars

During her youth in a provincial castle town at the rise of militant Imperialism and, later, as a young, self-taught artist on the fringe of Tokyo's avant-garde during the mid-'50s, Yayoi Kusama developed a private form of protest against the repressive environment of prewar and wartime Japan. Determinedly pursuing an independent vision, she disparaged the Japanese art bureaucracy for its "authoritative and narrow-minded" ways. In 1958, at the age of twenty-seven, she moved to New York to search for fame and fortune—hundreds of others would soon follow. Georgia O'Keeffe, with whom Kusama had established a correspondence from Japan, was puzzled by her young admirer and responded, "It seems to me very odd that you are so ambitious to show your paintings here..." What O'Keeffe could not perceive at the time, however, was Kusama's troubled remove from banal experience and the intensity of her obsession with expressing her psychic life through art.

Diagnosed as a young woman with an obsessive-compulsive and hysterical condition, Kusama—who has been resident in a psychiatric institution in Tokyo since 1977—attributes her manic obsession with themes of repetition, aggregation, and accumulation to a recurring hallucination she first experienced as a child:

> One day I was looking at the red flower patterns of the tablecloth on a table, and when I looked up I saw the same pattern covering the ceiling, the windows, and the walls, and finally all over the room, my body, and the universe. I felt as if I had begun to self-obliterate, to revolve in the infinity of endless time and the absoluteness of space, and be reduced to nothingness....

Throughout Kusama's life-work, in media ranging from small watercolors to large-scale oil paintings, from single *objets* to room-size environments, from studio "orgies" to naked demonstrations in the streets of lower Manhattan, she has used single units to construct repetitive patterns—such as the arcs composing her *Infinity Nets* paintings, the sewn-and-stuffed-cloth phallic forms covering found domestic objects in her *Accumulation* and *Compulsion Furniture* series, and later the polka dots she painted on the bodies of those who participated in her free-love, anti-war Happenings of the (*cont'd on p. 41*)

Right: Yayoi Kusama with works from her *Driving Image* series, c. 1962.

Farewell Supper, 1981. Mixed media, 44 ¾ x 132 ½ x 101 ½ in.

Right: Yayoi Kusama with *My Flower Bed* in her studio, probably on East 14th Street, N.Y.C., c. 1965–66.

Mirror Room (Pumpkin), interior view, 1991. Mixed media, 78 x 78 x 78 in.

Left: Yayoi Kusama with *Mirror Room (Pumpkin)*, installation view, The Hara Museum, Tokyo.

Violet Obsession, 1994. Mixed media, 39 x 149 x 72 in.

Six Guests, 1985. Mixed media, 72 x 50 ¾ x 44 in.

late 1960s. Kusama's fetishistic manipulation of the formal element to create serial, aggregate, or all-over styles (the multiple erect protuberances with which she transformed living room furniture, dressers, and kitchen utensils) aligned her—though she defied categorization—with the emergence of Pop, Op, Minimalism, and Psychedelic art in New York, and with monochrome painting and the Zero, Nul, and Nouveaux Réalistes groups in Europe.

Respected by many (including Joseph Cornell, who fixated on her) as the quintessential "artist's artist," Kusama often eluded the contemporary Euro-American art establishment and, when she returned to Japan in 1972, critics there were also slow to recognize her genius. Yoshiaki Tōno, an influential critic of the postwar generation, acknowledged that Kusama was "handicapped" because, as he remarked once, "She's Japanese, she's a woman, she's an artist, and she's avant-garde. These are the worst conditions."

Over the last decade, there has been an active revival of interest in Kusama's work. Whereas, in 1966, Italian officials had threatened her for crashing the Venice Biennale with an outdoor installation of 1,500 mirror balls (which Kusama surreptitiously sold for $2 each), in 1993, she was the first artist ever to be selected as Japan's sole representative for this prestigious international show. Following Emperor Hirohito's death in 1989, the will to challenge the oppressive social taboos surrounding *tennosei*—the modern emperor system—made the radical '60s a nostalgic topic of public discourse in Japan, and younger Japanese artists found a model in Kusama, whose outrageous postures have always expressed the romantic spirit of radical will.

In recent years, Kusama's preoccupation with sex, madness, and death by "self-obliteration" has also attracted theorists of Outside Art and feminist art history. Many have interpreted Kusama's relentless and aggregate use of the phallus as the aggressive will to defy oppressive male power by possessing it symbolically herself; long before the term "feminist art" was coined, however, outrage against authoritative male regimes defined Kusama's art-making. But her most profound defiance is not directed outward to the political world of systems and hierarchies. It is, rather, directed at the terror of her own being. By giving her fantastic vision lucid form, she proves the power of creative will over the self's ever-degenerative impulses.

—Alexandra Munroe

Left: *Sea (B)*, 1985. Mixed media, 30 x 20 x 10 ½ in.

Madame Edwarda

The following story appeared in Paris under the pseudonym Pierre Angélique in two small underground editions in 1941 and 1945. It was finally published under Bataille's own name by the publishing house of Jean-Jacques Pauvert in 1956. This translation first appeared in The Evergreen Review *in 1964, and is reprinted here in tribute to Barney Rosset, in recognition of his daring editorial vision.*

•

Anguish only is sovereign absolute. The sovereign is a king no more: it dwells low-hiding in big cities. It knits itself up in silence, obscuring its sorrow. Crouching thick-wrapped, there it waits, lies waiting for the advent of him who shall strike a general terror; but meanwhile and even so its sorrow scornfully mocks at all that comes to pass, at all there is.

There—I had come to a street corner—there a foul dizzying anguish got its nails into me (perhaps because I'd been staring at a pair of furtive whores sneaking down the stair of a urinal). A great urge to heave myself dry always comes over me at such moments. I feel I have got to make myself naked, or strip naked the whores I covet: it's in stale flesh's tepid warmth I always suppose I'll find relief. But this time I soothed my guts with the weaker remedy: I asked for a pernod at the counter, drank the glass in one gulp, and then went on and on, from zinc counter to zinc counter drinking until … The night was done falling.

I began to wander among those streets—the propitious ones— which run between the Boulevard Poissonnière and the Rue Saint-Denis. Loneliness and the dark strung my drunken excitement tighter and tighter. I wanted to be laid as bare as was the night there in those empty streets: I slipped off my pants and moved on, carrying them draped over my arm. Numb, I coasted on a wave of overpowering freedom, I sensed that I'd got bigger. In my hand I held my straight-risen sex.

(The beginning is tough. My way of telling about these things is raw. I could have avoided that and still made it sound plausible. It would have seemed "likely," detours would have been to my advantage. But this is how it has to be, there is no beginning by scuttling in sideways. I continue … and it gets tougher.)

Not wanting trouble, I got back into my pants and headed toward the Mirrors. I entered the place and found myself in the light again. Amidst a swarm of girls, Madame Edwarda, naked, looked bored to death. Ravishing, she was the sort I had a taste for. So I picked her. She came and sat down beside me. I hardly took the time to reply when the waiter asked what it was to be, I clutched Edwarda, she surrendered herself: our two mouths met in a sickly kiss. The room was packed with men and women, and that was the wasteland where the game was played. Then, at a certain moment, her hand slid, I burst suddenly, like a pane of glass shattering, flooding my clothes. My hands were holding Madame Edwarda's buttocks and I felt her break in two at the same instant: and in her starting, roving eyes, terror, and in her throat, a long-drawn whistled rasp.

Then I remembered my desire for infamy, or rather that it was infamous I had at all costs to be. I made out laughter filtering through the tumult of voices, of glare, of smoke. But nothing mattered anymore. I squeezed Edwarda in my arms; immediately, icebound, I felt smitten within by a new shock. From very high above, a kind of stillness swept down upon me and froze me. It was as though I were borne aloft in a flight of headless and unbodied angels shaped from the broad swooping of wings, but it was simpler than that. I became unhappy and felt painfully forsaken, as one is when in the presence of GOD. It was worse and more of a letdown than too much to drink. And right away I was filled with unbearable sadness to think that this very grandeur descending upon me was withering away the pleasure I hoped to have with Edwarda.

I told myself I was being ridiculous. Edwarda and I having exchanged not one word, I was assailed by a huge uneasiness. I couldn't breathe so much as a hint of the state I was in, a wintry night had locked round me. Struggling, I wanted to kick the table and send the glasses flying to raise the bloody roof, but that table wouldn't budge, it must have been bolted to the floor. I don't suppose a drunk can ever have to face anything more comical. Everything swam out of sight. Madame Edwarda was gone, so was the room.

I was pulled out of my dazed confusion by an only too human voice. Madame Edwarda's thin voice, like her slender body, was obscene: "I guess what you want is to see the old rag and ruin," she said. Hanging on to the tabletop with both hands, I twisted around toward her. She was seated, she held one leg stuck up in the air, to open her crack yet wider she used fingers to draw the folds of skin apart. And so Madame Edwarda's "old rag and ruin" lowered at me, hairy and pink, just as full of life as some loathsome squid. "Why," I stammered in a subdued tone, "why are you doing that?" "You can see for yourself," she said, "I'm GOD." "I'm going crazy—" "Oh, no you don't, you've got to see, look …" Her harsh, scraping voice mellowed, she became almost childlike in order to say, with a lassitude, with the infinite smile of abandon: "Oh, listen, fellow! The fun I've had …"

She had not shifted from her position, her leg was still cocked in the air. And her tone was commanding: "Come here." "Do you mean," I protested, "in front of all these people?" "Sure," she said, "why not?" I was shaking, I looked at her: motionless, she smiled back so sweetly that I shook. At last, reeling, I sank down on my knees and feverishly pressed my lips to that running, teeming wound. Her bare thigh caressingly nudged my ear, I thought I heard a sound of roaring sea-surge, it is the same sound you hear when you put your ear to a large conch shell. In the brothel's boisterous chaos and in the atmosphere of corroding absurdity I was breathing (it seemed to me that I was choking, I was flushed, I was sweating) I hung strangely suspended, quite as though at that same point we,

Edwarda and I, were losing ourselves in a wind-freighted night, on the edge of the ocean.

I heard another voice, a woman's but mannish. She was a robust and handsome person, respectably got up. "Well now, my children," in an easy, deep tone, "up you go." The second-in-command of the house collected my money. I rose and followed Madame Edwarda whose tranquil nakedness was already traversing the room. But this so ordinary passage between the close-set tables, through the dense press of clients and girls, this vulgar ritual of "the lady going up" with the man who wants her in tow, was, at that moment, nothing short of an hallucinating solemnity for me: Madame Edwarda's sharp heels clicking on the tiled floor, the smooth advance of her long obscene body, the acrid smell I drank in, the smell of a woman in the throes of joy, of that pale body ... Madame Edwarda went on ahead of me, raised up unto the very clouds ... The room's noisy unheeding of her happiness, of the measured gravity of her step, was royal consecration and triumphal holiday: death itself was guest at the feast, was there in what whorehouse nudity terms the pig-sticker's stab . . . .
. . . .
. . . . the mirrors, wherewith the room's walls were every-where sheathed and the ceiling too, cast multiple reflections of an animal coupling, but, at each least movement, our bursting hearts would strain wide open to welcome "the emptiness of heaven."

Making that love liberated us at last. On our feet, we stood gaz-ing soberly at each other: Madame Edwarda held me spellbound, never had I seen a prettier girl—nor one more naked. Her eyes fastened steadily upon me, she removed a pair of white silk stockings from a bureau drawer, she sat on the edge of the bed and drew them on. The delirious joy of being naked possessed her: once again she parted her legs, opened her crack, the pungent odor of her flesh and mine commingled flung us both into the same heart's utter exhaustion. She put on a white bolero, beneath a domino cloak she disguised her nakedness. The domino's hood cowled her head, a black velvet mask, fitted with a beard of lace, hid her face. So arrayed, she sprang away from me, saying: "Now let's go."

"Go? Do they let you go out?" I asked. "Hurry up, Fifi," she replied gaily, "you can't go out undressed." She tossed me my clothes and helped me climb into them, and as she did so, from her caprice, there now and then passed a sly exchange, a nasty little wink between her flesh and mine. We went down a narrow stairway, encountered nobody but the chambermaid. Brought to a halt by the abrupt darkness of the street, I was startled to discover Edwarda rushing away, swathed in black. She ran, eluded me, was off, the mask she wore was turning her into an animal. Though the air wasn't cold, I shivered. Edwarda, something alien; above our heads, a starry sky, mad and void. I thought I was going to stagger, to fall, but didn't, and kept walking.

At that hour of the night the street was deserted. Suddenly gone wild, mute, Edwarda raced on alone. The Porte Saint-Denis loomed before her, she stopped. I stopped too, she waited for me underneath the arch—unmoving, exactly under the arch. She was entirely black, simply there, as distressing as an emptiness, a hole. I realized she wasn't frolicking, wasn't joking, and indeed that, beneath the garment enfolding her, she was mindless: rapt, absent. Then all the drunken exhilaration drained out of me, then I knew that She had not lied, that She was GOD. Her presence had about it the unintelligible out-and-out simplicity of a stone— right in the middle of the city I had the feeling of being in the mountains at nighttime, lost in a lifeless, hollow solitude.

I felt that I was free of Her—I was alone, as if face to face with black rock. I trembled, seeing before me what in all this world is most barren, most bleak. In no way did the comic horror of my situation escape me: She, the sight of whom petrified me now, the instant before had ... And the transformation had occurred in the way something glides. In Madame Edwarda, grief—a grief without tears or pain—had glided into a vacant silence. Nonetheless, I wanted to find out: this woman, so naked just a moment ago, who lightheartedly had called me "Fifi" ... I crossed in her direction, anguish warned me to go no farther, but I didn't stop.

Unspeaking, she slipped away, retreating toward the pillar on the left. Two paces separated me from that monumental gate, when I passed under the stone overhead, the domino vanished soundlessly. I paused, listening, holding my breath. I was amazed that I could grasp it all so clearly: when she had run off I had known that, no matter what, she had had to run, to dash under the arch, and when she had stopped, that she had been hung in a sort of trance, an absence, far out of range and beyond the possibility of any laughter. I couldn't see her any longer: a deathly darkness sank down from the vault. Without having given it a second's thought, I *knew* that a season of agony was beginning for me. I consented to suffer, I desired to suffer, to go farther, as far as the "emptiness" itself, even were I to be stricken, destroyed, no matter. I knew, I wanted that knowing, for I lusted after her secret and did not for one instant doubt that it was death's kingdom.

I moaned underneath the stone roof, then, terrified, I laughed: "Of all men, the sole to traverse the nothingness of this arch!" I trembled at the thought she might fly, vanish forever. I trembled as I accepted that, but from imagining it I became crazed: I leaped to the pillar and spun round it. As quickly I circled the other pillar on the right: she was gone. But I couldn't believe it. I remained woestruck before the portal and I was sinking into the last despair when upon the far side of the avenue I spied the domino, immobile, just faintly visible in the shadow: she was standing upright, entranced still, planted in front of the ranged tables and chairs of a café shut up for the night. I drew near her: she seemed gone out of her mind, some foreign existence, the creature apparently of another world and, in the streets of this one, less than a phantom, less than a lingering mist. Softly she withdrew before me until in her retreat she touched against a table on the empty terrace. A little noise. As if I had waked her, in a lifeless voice she inquired: "Where am I?"

Desperate, I pointed to the empty sky curved above us. She looked up and for a brief moment stood still, her eyes vague behind the mask, her gaze lost in the fields of stars. I supported her, it was in an unhealthy way that she was clutching the domino, with both hands pulling it tight around her. She began to shake, to convulse. She was suffering. I thought she was crying but it was as if the world and the distress in her, strangling her, were preventing her from giving way to sobs. She wrenched away from me, gripped by a shapeless disgust; suddenly lunatic, she darted forward, stopped short, whirled her cloak high, displayed her behind, snapped her rump up with a quick jerk of her spine, then came back and hurled herself at me. A gale of dark savagery blew up inside her, raging, she tore and hammered at my face, hit with clenched fists, swept away by a demented impulse to violence. I tottered and fell. She fled.

I was still getting to my feet—was actually still on my knees—when she returned. She shouted in a raveled, impossible voice, she screamed at the sky and, horrified, her whirling arms flailing at vacant air: "I can't stand any more," she shrilled, "but you, you fake priest. I shit on you—" That broken voice ended in a rattle, her outstretched hands groped blindly, then she collapsed.

Down, she writhed, shaken by respiratory spasms. I bent over her and had to rip the lace from the mask, for she was chewing and trying to swallow it. Her thrashings had left her naked, her breasts spilled through her bolero ... I saw her flat, pallid belly, and above her stockings, her hairy crack yawned astart. This nakedness now had the absence of meaning and at the same time the overabundant meaning of death-shrouds. Strangest of all—and most disturbing—was the silence that ensnared Edwarda—owing to the pain she was in, further communication was impossible and I let myself be absorbed into this unutterable barrenness—into this black night hour of the being's core no less a desert nor less hostile than the empty skies. The way her body flopped like a fish, the ignoble rage expressed by the ill written on her features, cindered the life in me, dried it down to the lees of revulsion.

(Let me explain myself. No use laying it all up to irony when I say of Madame Edwarda that she is GOD. But GOD figured as a public whore and gone crazy—that, viewed through the optic of "philosophy," makes no sense at all. I don't mind having my sorrow derided if derided it has to be, he only will grasp me aright whose heart holds a wound that is an incurable wound, who never, for anything, in any way, would be cured of it ... And what man, if so wounded, would ever be willing to "die" of any other hurt?)

The awareness of my irreparable doom whilst, in that night, I knelt next to Edwarda was not less clear and not less imposing than it is now, as I write. Edwarda's sufferings dwelt in me like the quick truth of an arrow: one knows it will pierce the heart, but death will ride in with it. As I waited for annihilation, all that subsisted in me seemed to me to be the dross over which man's life tarries. Squared against a silence so black, something leaped in my heavy despair's midst. Edwarda's convulsions snatched me away from my own self, they cast my life into a desert waste "beyond," they cast it there carelessly, callously, the way one flings a living body to the hangman.

A man condemned to die, when after long hours of waiting he

arrives in broad daylight at the exact spot the horror is to be wrought, observes the preparations, his too full heart beats as though to burst; upon the narrow horizon which is his, every object, every face is clad in weightiest meaning and helps tighten the vise whence there is no time left him to escape. When I saw Madame Edwarda writhing on the pavement, I entered a similar state of absorption, but I did not feel imprisoned by the change that occurred in me. The horizon before which Edwarda's sickness placed me was a fugitive one, fleeing like the object anguish seeks to attain. Torn apart, a certain power welled up in me, a power that would be mine upon condition I agreed to hate myself. Ugliness was invading all of me. The vertiginous sliding which was tipping me into ruin had opened up a prospect of indifference; of concerns, of desires there was no longer any question; at this point, the fever's desiccating ecstasy was issuing out of my utter inability to check myself.

(If you have to lay yourself bare, then you cannot play with words, trifle with slow-marching sentences. Should no one unclothe what I have said, I shall have written in vain. Edwarda is no dream's airy invention, the real sweat of her body soaked my handkerchief, so real was she that, led on by her, I came to want to do the leading in my turn. This book has its secret, I may not disclose it. Now more words.)

Finally, the crisis subsided. Her convulsions continued a little longer, but with waning fury, she began to breathe again, her features relaxed, ceased to be hideous. Drained entirely of strength, I lay full length down on the roadway beside her. I covered her with my clothing. She was not heavy and I decided to pick her up and carry her. One of the boulevard taxi stands was not far away. She lay unstirring in my arms. It took time to get there, thrice I had to pause and rest. She came back to life as we moved along and when we reached the place she wanted to be set down. She took a step and swayed. I caught her, held her; held by me she got into the cab. Weakly, she said: "… not yet … tell him to wait." I told the driver to wait. Half-dead from weariness, I climbed in too and slumped down beside Edwarda.

For a long time we remained without saying anything. Madame Edwarda, the driver and I, not budging in our seats, as though the taxi were rolling ahead. At last Edwarda spoke to me. "I want him to take us to Les Halles." I repeated her instructions to the driver, and we started off. He took us through dimly lit streets. Calm and deliberate, Edwarda loosened the ties of her cloak, it fell away from her. She got rid of the mask too, she removed her bolero and, for her own hearing, murmured: "Naked as a beast." She rapped on the glass partition, had the cab stop, and got out. She walked round to the driver and when close enough to touch him, said: "You see … I'm bare-assed, Jack. Let's fuck." Unmoving, the driver looked at that beast. Having backed off a short distance, she had raised her left leg, eager to show him her crack. Without a word and unhurriedly, the man stepped out of the car. He was thickset, solidly built. Edwarda twined herself around him, fastened her mouth upon his, and with one hand scouted about in his underwear. It was a long heavy member she dragged through his fly. She eased his trousers down to his ankles. "Come into the back seat," she told him. He sat down next to me. Stepping in after him, she mounted and straddled him. Carried away by voluptuousness, with her own hands she stuffed the hard stave into her hole. I sat there, lifeless and watching: her slithering movements were slow and cunning and plainly she gleaned a nerve-snapping pleasure from them. The driver retaliated, struggling with brute heaving vigor; bred of their naked bodies' intimacy, little by little that embrace strained to the final pitch of excess at which the heart fails. The driver fell back, spent and near to swooning. I switched on the overhead light in the taxi. Edwarda sat bolt upright astride the still stiff member, her head angled sharply back, her hair straying loose. Supporting her nape, I looked into her eyes: they gleamed white. She pressed against the hand that was holding her up, the tension thickened the wail in her throat. Her eyes swung to rights and then she seemed to grow easy. She saw me, from her stare, then, at that moment, I knew she was drifting home from the "impossible" and in her nether depths I could discern a dizzying fixity. The milky outpouring traveling through her, the jet spitting from the root, flooding her with joy, came spurting out again in her very tears: burning tears streamed from her wide-open eyes. Love was dead in those eyes, they contained a daybreak aureate chill, a transparency wherein I read death's letters. And everything swam drowned in that dreaming stare: a long member, stubby fingers prying open fragile flesh, my anguish, and the recollection of scum-flecked lips—there was nothing which didn't contribute to that blind dying into extinction.

Edwarda's pleasure—fountain of boiling water, heartbursting furious tide-flow—went on and on, weirdly, unendingly; that stream of luxury, its strident inflection, glorified her being unceasingly, made her nakedness unceasingly more naked, her lewdness ever more intimate. Her body, her face swept in ecstasy were abandoned to the unspeakable coursing and ebbing, in her sweetness there hovered a crooked smile: she saw me to the bottom of my dryness, from the bottom of my desolation I sensed her joy's torrent run free. My anguish resisted the pleasure I ought to have sought. Edwarda's pain-wrung pleasure filled me with an exhausting impression: of bearing witness to a miracle. My own distress and fever seemed small things to me. But that was what I felt, those are the only great things in me which gave answer to the rapture of her whom in the deeps of an icy silence I called "my heart."

Some last shudders took slow hold of her, then her sweat-bathed frame relaxed—and there in the darkness sprawled the driver, felled by his spasm. I still held Edwarda up, my hand still behind her head, the stave slipped out, I helped her lie down, wiped her wet body. Her eyes dead, she offered no resistance. I had switched off the light, she was half asleep, like a drowsy child. The same sleepiness must have borne down upon the three of us, Edwarda, the driver, and me.

(Continue? I meant to. But I don't care now. I've lost interest. I put down what oppresses me at the moment of writing: Would it all be absurd? Or might it make some kind of sense? I've made myself sick wondering about it. I awake in the morning—just the way millions do, millions of boys and girls, infants and old men, their slumbers dissipated forever . . . These millions, those slumbers have no meaning. A hidden meaning? Hidden, yes, "obviously!" But if nothing has any meaning, there's no point in my doing anything. I'll beg off. I'll use any deceitful means to get out of it, in the end I'll have to let go and sell myself to meaninglessness, nonsense: that is man's killer, the one who tortures and kills, not a glimmer of hope left. But if there is a meaning? Today I don't know what it is. Tomorrow? Tomorrow, who can tell? Am I going then to find out what it is? No, I can't conceive of any "meaning" other than "my" anguish, and as for that, I know all about it. And for the time being: nonsense. Monsieur Nonsense is writing and understands that he is mad. It's atrocious. But his madness, this meaninglessness—how "serious" it has become all of a sudden!—might that indeed be "meaningful"? [No, Hegel has nothing to do with a maniac girl's "apotheosis."] My life only has a meaning insofar as I lack one: oh, but let me be mad! Make something of all this he who is able to, understand it he who is dying, and there the living self is, knowing not why, its teeth chattering in the lashing wind: the immensity, the night engulfs it and, all on purpose, that living self is there just in order . . . "not to know." But as for GOD? What have you got to say, Monsieur Rhetorician? And you, Monsieur Godfearer?—GOD, if He knew, would be a swine.* O Thou my Lord [in my distress I call out unto my heart], O deliver me, make them blind! The story—how shall I go on with it?)

But I am done.

From out of the slumber which for so short a space kept us in the taxi, I awoke, the first to open his eyes . . . The rest is irony, long, weary waiting for death. . . .

Translated from the French by Austryn Wainhouse

---

* I said "GOD, if He knew would be a swine." He (He would I suppose be, at that particular moment, somewhat in disorder, his peruke would sit all askew) would entirely grasp the idea . . . but what would there be of the human about him? Beyond, beyond everything . . . and yet farther, and even farther still . . . HIM-SELF, in an ecstasy, above an emptiness . . . And now? I TREMBLE.

A Private Talk Among Friends

(The actor impersonates two women seated on stools. He has but to switch from one stool to the other and change shawls of distinctive design to alternate between the two. Their shoes should be in fashion, and their conversation that of women of the world in the swim of things. The setting is a private house.)

KORITTO
(Welcoming her friend, who has come to visit.)
Do have a seat, Metro.
(Realizes that there is none. Wheels on her servant girl, shouting and making hysterical gestures with her arms.)
                                    Get up! A stool
For this lady! Must I say what to do
Or you don't lift a finger? Is that it?
Are you some kind of rock, or a servant?
The liveliness of a corpse! Except, of course,
When I measure out your ration of meal.
You count the grains. If I spill a little,
You grumble and pout until I wonder
The walls don't sigh in sympathy and fall.
(Ominous pause. Finds new angle of attack.)
Just now wiping the stool clean, aren't you?
And why, pray, hasn't it been kept dusted?
You can be very thankful there's a guest,
Else wouldn't you taste the flat of my hand!

METRO

(Sympathetically, complacently.)

We wear the same yoke, my dear Koritto.

I have to bark like a dog day and night

At these lazy and unspeakable oafs.

(Pulls her stool closer.)

What I've come about . . .

KORITTO

(Suddenly jumps up and runs toward the servants, flapping her dress.)

Out from underfoot, all you shiftless sluts!

You sneaks and gossips! All ears and tongues

And nothing else to you but idle butts!

(Sits. Composes herself.)

METRO

(Tries again.)

You must tell me now,

Koritto dear, who made you your dildo*,

the beautifully stitched red leather one.

KORITTO

(Agape with surprise.)

But how now, when, where can you have seen it?

METRO

Erinna's daughter had it given to her

Day before yesterday, Nossis, you know.

What a beautiful present for a girl.

KORITTO

(Befuddled and alarmed.)

Nossis? Who gave it to her?

---

* The Greek is *baubon*, a leather penis for masturbation.
  The word means "a pacifier."

METRO

                           If I tell,

Will you tell on me?

KORITTO

(Touching her eyelids with her fingers.)

                        These sweet eyes, Metro!

Koritto's mouth lets out naught.

METRO

                       Euboulé,

Bitas's wife, gave it to her. Promised her,

What's more, nobody would be the wiser.

KORITTO

Women! That woman will uproot me yet.

I let her have it because she begged me.

Metro, I haven't yet used it myself!

And she treats it like something she has found,

And makes an improper present of it.

Goodbye and goodbye to a friend like her,

Is what I say. She can find other friends.

She has lent my property to Nossis!

Adresteia forgive me for speaking

Stronger than a woman should. But Nossis!

I wouldn't give her my old worn-out one

Even if I still had a thousand more.

METRO

Now, now, Koritto. Keep your dander down.

Better to enjoy an even temper.

I shouldn't have babbled. I talk too much.

It would be an improvement all around

Were I to lose my tongue. But, to get back,

Who did make it? Do tell me as a friend.
(Taken aback a bit.)
Why are you looking at me so funny?
I'm Metro, not a stranger, after all.
What is this prudishness? Be a sport now.
Who's the craftsman that made it? What's his name?

KORITTO
(Laughing.)
What a pitiful plea! Kerdon made it!

METRO
Which Kerdon? The gray-eyed one, the Kerdon
Who's Kylaithis Myrtalinê's neighbor?
He couldn't make a plectrum for a harp.
Near Hermodoros's apartment house
Off Main Street, there's another, somebody
In his day but getting old, I would think.
He used to do it with Pylaithis when
She was living. Gone but not forgotten,
Poor dear, if her kin ever think of her.

KORITTO
Neither of those, Metro, as you've figured.
This one is Khian or Erythraian,
One or the other, baldheaded and little.
He is the spitting image of Prexinos
But talks altogether different, though.
He does his work at home behind closed doors,
You never know where revenue spies lurk.
Real Khoan, his stitching and polishing.
You'd think Athena had done it, not Kerdon.
Well, I—he brought me two of them, Metro—
I thought my eyes would pop out with staring.

I can tell you this, we are all alone,
No man was ever hung like these beauties,
So long and stiff, and as smooth as a dream,
And the leather straps are as soft as wool.
What a godsend to women, this cobbler!

METRO
Why didn't you buy the other one too?

KORITTO
What didn't I do to get it, Metro!
I tried every persuasion, I kissed him,
Fondled his bald head, gave him a sweet drink,
Called him my pet, tickled his hairy ears,
Everything but open my legs to him.

METRO
But you should have, if that's what he wanted.

KORITTO
Yes, but I really didn't have the chance.
Bitas's Euboulé was here grinding meal
On my millstone, as she does day and night,
Wearing it out, I'll need a new one soon,
I swear, Bitas being too tightfisted
To spend four obols for one of his own.

METRO
How did he know to come here, Koritto?
Don't fib.

KORITTO
                    Artemis sent him, Kandas's wife,
She showed him my house.

METRO

Aiei! Artemis,
She's always into things, more than Thallo,
Especially with anything sexy.
But if he wouldn't sell you both of them,
Didn't you ask who ordered the other?

KORITTO

Yes I did. He wasn't about to tell.
Somebody he hopes to seduce, I'll vow.

METRO

(Rising, arranging her shawl for the street.)
Well, I think I'd better be leaving you.
I just might happen upon Artemis
And find out when I can find Kerdon in.
(Blows a kiss.)
Wish me luck, Koritto.
(Breaks into a salacious grin.)
                              A sweet longing
Buzzes around in a certain person.
(Leaves.)

KORITTO

(To a servant.)
Go close the front door, you fool of a girl,
And then go count the chickens in the yard,
And throw them some darnel while you're there.
People steal anything nowadays, for sure,
Even your pet hen and her on your lap.

Translated from the Greek by Guy Davenport

Last Things

The simplest sort of horror story (and the most gratifying somehow) starts with the damage—something ruined in ways too peculiar to explain, glimpsed, say, at high speed along a country highway at dusk just at that rosy half-lit moment before one flips on the headlights: little jerks of their eyes now to the right—hers then his but then it's gone and they fall silent watching the pink light leaving the tops of the pines; he looks back once in the mirror but everything's shadowy against the sky like one of those black-and-orange silhouette landscapes schoolchildren produce at Halloween—such an easy effect yet so dramatic with all the particulars of the world hopelessly lost in the radiance.

"Was that a scarecrow?" she says at last. And now the fact acquires a presence, seems to accompany them into the gathering dark, uphill and down along the blacktop with the pine trees closing in, losing all particularity. She watches his face now, how it brightens in the glow from the rearview mirror at the top of every hill but more and more faintly each time. She has to remind him about the headlights.

"Was that a scarecrow?" she asks again. He shakes his head the way he might at her concern for something dead in the road, some poor domestic animal—although in that case she wouldn't have said anything except, "Oh dear," perhaps, bringing her hand to her face and glancing over to see his expression. Then, if he sensed her looking, he might shake his head and that would be that; but now it's unreasonable, she feels, inconsistent—she felt his foot come off the pedal, caught the deflection of his eyes. She looks behind for headlights, twists around, and watches for a while the little lavender-gray slot of sky where the pine trees converge, hoping for someone else who might be observed to have passed the same spot and might be felt to intervene as it were, to interrupt the continuity and development of her thoughts, represent the succession of ordinary events across the moment, distributing it, delegating it in a sense. A couple of times she imagines a faint preliminary glow, a subtle brightening to the sky above the road but there's nothing further and presently she turns back around, sole custodian of what she now seeks to reevaluate in terms consistent with her husband's response: something dead, run over, and tossed up onto a fence or a bush somehow, not a person but a deer, maybe a dog flattened by the impact like in a cartoon, unfolded, ears out sideways like a hat, all spread out and presented rose-colored in the sunlight in the corner of her eye, a scatter of teeth across its face.

He's shaking his head again very slightly.

"What?" she says.

He flicks on the brights, which she dislikes along this stretch with the pines so close on either side because it seems so strongly to anticipate some sort of panicky event. Like shining a flashlight under one's bed when one was little, she imagines. He's flicking them off and on at the car that's been intermittently beaming over the rises, practically blinding now as it approaches, zooming past, hauling a boat at an alarming rate of speed. She turns to look, watching the taillights disappear and reappear, testing her sense of it and whether, even traveling in the wrong direction, it might serve her purpose, blowing past that spot in the dark, shaking the trees, and ablating the fact to some extent.

"So what was it really?" She turns back around. The road's bending off to the right and the brights are shining into the pine trees, faintly scanning across like a searchlight. She looks down. He's going to tease her, she suspects.

"If not a scarecrow?"

"Right." She closes her eyes.

"Well, just because you've got your category 'scarecrows'—let's call it a set—doesn't mean that under certain conditions, in the darkest recesses of the heart . . ." He pauses, turns and looks at her now; she senses it, opens her eyes, and he's glancing over and smiling.

"What?" she says after a second, letting the question float away. He's doing something with his seatbelt, unfastening it finally and leaning back with his arms out straight, both hands on top of the wheel. The forest opens up now into meadow on either side, pale cattle here and there which, except for a couple right by the road, are hardly visible upon approach but as they are passed become luminous, their east sides lit by a nearly full moon just clearing the tree line. She brings her face up against the window, cupping her hands around her eyes to watch the effect, the materialization cow by cow or sometimes several at once sort of rippling into visibility across the meadow into the distance, all standing, head down to the grass in that posture one associates with cows, that represents their passiveness, their essential permanence and receptivity, here presented out of the darkness one after another in such a spectral display, such a marvelous reiteration it takes away her breath for a moment, seems to absorb and neutralize her concerns altogether as if each glowing animal accompanied her like headlights past that critical point, as if all one's unpleasant thoughts in fact might be subordinate to a field of cattle in the moonlight. A rush of trees and everything's dark except for the moon itself peeking through like code—dots to dashes—now longer streaks as the woods start to thin, about to open up again, she hopes, onto pasture, a few more cattle perhaps just to establish the sense of them, or their luminosity at least, as an extended phenomenon like an aurora or a rainbow, something serene and transcendent like that, like a glimpse of the ocean to restore calm and lend perspective. The moon sweeps free of the trees, out over the meadow which is black as felt—some sort of thick low cover like rye grass or alfalfa—but no cows, not a glimmer. She wipes the window and looks again, holding her breath to keep from fogging the glass, extending her attention to every peripheral possibility the way one might hold oneself, jar in hand, toward the possibility of fireflies.

She turns away after a minute; the woods close in again; the high beams are shooting off between the trees, in anticipation, she feels, of something darting across, lurching suddenly out of the woods into their path any second.

"It wasn't a deer," she says quietly. She looks over and he shrugs. A fall of yellow oak or sweet gum leaves swirls out of the dark across the headlights. The car rocks slightly with the wind. "It wasn't a deer," she says again just as quietly, looking down into her purse which she has lifted into her lap, fishing around now as if for evidence, withdrawing a probably empty Chiclets box which she squeezes and taps against her palm to dislodge any pieces that might be stuck.

"You know?" She looks over at her husband again, tapping the box a few more times, then stripping off the cellophane, and starting to tear it from the top. "It looked like a person." She has it peeled apart now like a banana, laid out along its seams, nothing inside. "Didn't you think so?"

He glances over: "What have you got?"

She looks down at the box, holds it up by the corner, bringing her other hand to her face, unable to say anything for a moment, entirely surprised by her reaction to this: her operations upon the cardboard box, its inside-outness a sort of delicate indecency like a euphemism, like one of those naked female ivory dolls once provided to Chinese physicians to represent the unapproachable aristocratic sufferer—"Is there pain here?" he points and the answer comes from beyond the curtain, disembodied and, thus, inconceivably painful, unimaginably distant, like something howling in the woods.

"No more Chiclets," she says.

"No indeed," he replies.

Escapology

A shallow cut lets the blood bead:
and you could charm red bracelets,
coax necklaces from nowhere.
You stashed blades like savings,
pulled them out with a flourish
in a fan of silver.

Soon it was ribbons from the wrist
and sawing yourself in two; always
trying to disappear.
Then the finale: sedatives, restraints,
the escape-proof box. And you
lying there. A locked knife.

A Decomposition

The horse decoded on the killing floor:
a riddle of hair and bone
unknotted here
by a bad fall,
a buzzard, some
unkindness of ravens.
Then dogs came
for the dismantling:
splayed the legs to cord and cable,
emptied the chest,
snapped the brooches of the back.
The forelock sits
intact on the skull's crown,
like a wig;
the head's cockpit
fizzing with maggots.
The horse drones.

Three days later,
a bone rebus;
the horse is parsed.
The ribs at sail, the body like a boat
in a surf of horsehair,
hollowed, resonant.
The wind's knife wedged in the keys
of an organ and left; the horse
playing itself, its singular note, its cipher.
A signature, legible and bold.

BOB FLANAGAN

Visiting Hours

IN COLLABORATION WITH SHEREE ROSE

In 1992, Bob Flanagan's *Visiting Hours* transformed a space at the Santa Monica Museum of Art into a medical clinic, replete with waiting-room furniture, potted plants and copies of *Highlights for Children* magazines. An anatomical doll dripped simulated mucus and sperm; a chest X-ray portrayed cloudy lungs and pierced nipples; pictures of Houdini and cartoon pigs appeared on the walls. A wall of 1,400 alphabet blocks had been painstakingly stacked so that the initials "SM" and "CF" (cystic fibrosis) were repeated intermittently between illustrations of medical equipment, tit clamps, butt plugs, glue guns, and needles. A video installation expanded on these allusions with bondage scenes culled from cartoons and Hollywood films. In the middle of the gallery, in a re-created hospital room, Flanagan, who suffers from cystic fibrosis, was the patient. A poemlike text which wrapped around the gallery walls enumerated his masochism's various inspirations: from childhood encounters with doctors and nuns to fantasies of discipline and torture.

During the six-week run of *Visiting Hours*, Flanagan was periodically pulled out of his bed and hoisted to the rafters by a rope and pulley. Dangling by his feet, his thin pale frame rose above the room like a ghostly jack-in-the-box, or a departing soul. It was an eerily lyrical image, intimating that the body's crude physicality and its poetry aren't mutually exclusive. Perhaps the most disconcerting element of *Visiting Hours* is the underlying implication that desire and disease share a common principle of contagion: like an epidemiologist's charts, the installation mapped out a pattern of infection that seemed to embrace much of Western culture.

Blurring the well-worn boundary between art and life, *Visiting Hours* was a truly social work: many visitors ended up chatting by the artist's sickbed, trading stories of illness and disease. Ironically, by subverting the clinical aura of the exhibition space, Flanagan was able to remind us of art's potentially therapeutic side effects. His work implied that it is possible to reclaim the perverse bodies that

Because it feels good; because it makes me come; because I'm sick; because there ▾

culture has stolen from us. The force of this argument, its ability to shake you loose from your moorings, springs from the work's poetry and unnerving wit, and the singular poignance of the artist's presence.

—Ralph Rugoff

much sickness; because I say **FUCK THE SICKNESS**; because I like the attention;

because I was different; because kids beat me up on the way to school; because I w

miliated by nuns; because of the forts we built and the things we did inside them;

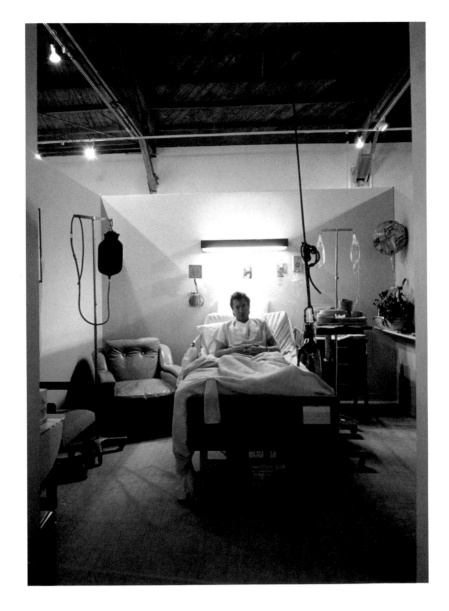

because of my genes; because of my parents; because they tied me to the crib so I would

t myself; because I had time to think; because I felt like I was going to die; because

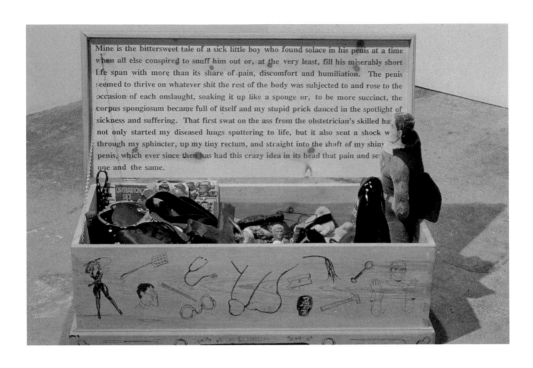

Mine is the bittersweet tale of a sick little boy who found solace in his penis at a time when all else conspired to snuff him out or, at the very least, fill his miserably short life span with more than its share of pain, discomfort and humiliation. The penis seemed to thrive on whatever shit the rest of the body was subjected to and rose to the occasion of each onslaught, soaking it up like a sponge or, to be more succinct, the corpus spongiosum became full of itself and my stupid prick danced in the spotlight of sickness and suffering. That first swat on the ass from the obstetrician's skilled ha not only started my diseased lungs sputtering to life, but it also sent a shock w through my sphincter, up my tiny rectum, and straight into the shaft of my shiny penis, which ever since then has had this crazy idea in its head that pain and se one and the same.

I'm a Catholic; because of "O" and how desperately I wanted to be her; because ha

Waiting Room, 1992. Chairs, table, rug, posters, assorted literature,
toys, games, and leather rose in vase.
p. 67

Installation view with (left to right): *Toy Box*, 1992; *CF/SM Alphabet Block Wall*,
1992; *Bob Flanagan's Chest X-rays with Nipple Rings*, 1992; *Bulletin Board*, 1992;
and *Wall of Pain*, 1981/92.
p. 68 (top)

CF/SM Alphabet Block Wall: 1,400 wooden blocks in nine sections
with three metal bars.
p. 68 (bottom)

Bulletin Board, 1992. Bulletin board, pushpins, photographs, drawings,
and newspaper clippings.
p. 69 (details)

Hospital Room (installation view with Bob Flanagan), 1992/94. Hospital bed,
medical equipment, chair, stool, bulletin board, linoleum flooring,
harness with pulley, food tray, TV, and video.
p. 70

Installation view with (left to right): *Visible Man*, 1992; *Wall of Pain*, 1981/92;
Sick Superman, 1992; and *Bob Flanagan's Chest X-rays with Nipple Rings*, 1992.
p. 71 (top)

Installation view with (clockwise from near left): *Potty Chair*, 1992;
Gurney of Nails, 1992; *Bob Flanagan's Sick*, 1991; *Hospital Entryway Wall
Installation* (detail), 1994; and *Sick Superman*, 1992.
p. 71 (bottom)

Toy Box, 1992. Silkscreen on wood with children's toys and bondage gear.
p. 72 (top)

e stores give me hard-ons; BECAUSE YOU ALWAYS HURT THE ONE YOU LOVE.

Video Casket, 1994. Coffin, embroidery, stand with draping, VCR, and live video
surveillance feed.
p. 72 (bottom)

Fetish

I have in my possession
an angel's wingbone—
valueless, I gather,
without the certificate
of authentication
which can only be signed by a bishop.

I treasure it, however,
and almost religiously love
the sweet feel of its curve
between thumb and forefinger
deep in my jacket pocket,
the way I'm fondling it now.

SAMUEL BECKETT

Eleuthéria

NOTES BY JOHN MONTAGUE AND BARNEY ROSSET

Sordid Inertia

I see a schoolboy when I think of him, said Yeats, referring to Keats and his delight in sensuous images, like sweetmeats. I see a student when I think of the young Beckett, a disreputable, down-at-the-heels "Trinity Scholard," with a fag at the lip, and a bottle of stout projecting from his soiled raincoat pocket. This malcontent is the central character in *A Dream of Fair to Middling Women* and *More Pricks Than Kicks*, where his *taedium vitae* expresses itself in the series of dubious jokes and listless actions which also thickens the atmosphere of "sordid inertia" in Beckett's only three-act play *Eleuthéria*, written in 1947 and published only now, over his dead body.

Quail before the lengthy and peculiar cast of characters! We have the Krap family, Henri and Violette, and their good-for-nothing son, mockingly called Victor, whose bedsit dominates the larger part of the stage. Both the senior Kraps appropriately have pains in their respective butts—father Krap's will soon prove fatal. Madame Krap's sister has married Dr. Piouk (the dignified spelling does not disguise the reference to a favorite Dublin student practice, generally provoked by many pints of stout). His views on the human race are also emetic, since he would vomit it forth through contraception, homosexuality, abortion, and euthanasia. Madame Krap's bosom pal is Madame Meck, a name that echoes the French slang for a prostitute's "pimp," *son mec.* Aspiring to join this menagerie is Victor's fiancée, the "alluring" Olga Skunk, a salubrious name for a sweet-smelling slip of a girl, whose breasts and haunches are much admired by the randy, though dying, father Krap. The only partly normal members of the Krap household are its obsequious servants, who pad in and out, stage front, drawn out of their frozen politeness only when Henri Krap demands a kiss, or delivers a slap.

Ensconced in his chair, and slowed by pain, Krap reminds us irresistibly of Hamm, the cantankerous tyrant in *Endgame*. Indeed, much of the later Beckett is implicit in these rough pages. Krap is a writer of the "shit genre" whom "the Lord has flushed...out." His wife's demand—"What's to be done?"—is a war cry that dwindles into the opening lines of *Godot*. We are told that Victor lives by foraging in garbage cans, but we see him in bed, or, like Clov in

Endgame, going "back and forth in his stocking feet, ... from the window to the footlights...."

Beckett's beloved father was a draftsman, and his skill is perhaps reflected in his son's brilliantly claustrophobic stage directions, where the disorder of Victor's bedroom encroaches on the Kraps' morning room, as Beckett explains, like "the sullied into the clean, the sordid into the decent..." or, waxing more eloquent, "the high seas becoming the harbor basin." The whole play also reflects the anguish and tension between the still relatively young and totally unsuccessful Beckett and his worried family: like slug-a-bed Victor, the former had never "been either lighthearted or alive."

A few years later, Godot would become a household word, but Beckett's view of the world would not soften. Since he belonged, with Sophocles, to the select company of those who would prefer not to have been born, one suspects that Dr. Piouk's Swiftian prescriptions for the restriction of the human race are partly Beckett's own, and that his cryptic title *Eleuthéria* (Greek for "freedom") is the second cousin of "euthanasia."

However, Beckett, like Henri Krap, did not believe in suicide, "recoiling from the great cure, through a sense of decency, or through cowardice...." I remember a grimly humorous discussion I had with Beckett, in the early '70s, about disappearance, his best plan being a boat with a hole in the bottom. He gave a philosophic sigh and added, "It's legally impossible. The widow wouldn't inherit for seven years." I also remember standing with him at closing time outside a vast café on the Boulevard St. Michel, watching in admiration as the *clochards* emerged from the shadows to scavenge the dustbins. They worked with such economy and skill, they might have been following the stage directions for a Beckett play. From *Eleuthéria* onwards, the darkness and disorder Beckett had struggled with all his life would become the cornerstone of his art. Victor, gleaning the dustbins only to shamble home to his unmade bed, foreshadows all the hapless hoboes of Beckett's later work. No wonder his favorite animal was the mole, burrowing away happily in blind darkness!

—John Montague, April 1995.

In 1947, about two years before he wrote Waiting for Godot, *Samuel Beckett wrote his first known play,* Eleuthéria. *After repeated attempts to get the play produced, he put it aside and, for the next forty years, only a few scholars and close friends had access to the manuscript. In 1987, Beckett offered the play to his old friend and original U.S. publisher, Barney Rosset; but, after an attempt to translate* Eleuthéria *from the original French, the eighty-year-old playwright decided that it was an impossible task. After Beckett's death, Rosset returned to the play and spent several years trying to convince the executors of the Beckett estate that the work was not a* pièce ratée—*or failed work—but a finished work by one of the greatest writers of the century. Finally, Foxrock, the company Rosset and the publishers of Four Walls Eight Windows had founded expressly to publish the play, received permission from the estate, and the full text will be published in the summer of 1995. An excerpt from the play's first act appears below.*

●

An area of the morning room in the home of the Kraps.
Round table, four period chairs, club chair, floor lamp, wall lamp with shade.
A late afternoon in winter.
Madame Krap seated at the table.
Madame Krap motionless.
A knock. A silence. Another knock.

Mme. Krap	(With a start) Come in. (Enter Jacques. He holds out to Mme. Krap a tray bearing a calling card. She takes up the card, looks at it, puts it back on the tray) Well? (Jacques uncomprehending) Well? (Jacques uncomprehending) What brutishness! (Jacques lowers his head) I thought I told you I was not in for anybody, except for Madame Meck.
Jacques	Yes, Madame, but it's Madame—Madame's sister—so I thought—
Mme. Krap	My sister!
Jacques	Yes, Madame.
Mme. Krap	You're being impertinent. (Jacques lowers his head) Show me that card. (Jacques holds out the tray again, Mme. Krap takes up the card again) Since when does my sister go by the name of Madame Piouk?

Jacques	(Embarrassed) I think—
Mme. Krap	You think?
Jacques	If Madame was to turn the card over. (Mme. Krap turns the card over and reads)
Mme. Krap	Couldn't you have told me so at once?
Jacques	I beg Madame's pardon.
Mme. Krap	Don't be so humble. (Jacques silent) Think about your union.
Jacques	Madame is joking.
Mme. Krap	Have her come in. (Jacques goes) Send in Marie.
Jacques	Very good, Madame. (Exit. Mme. Krap motionless. Enter Jacques) Madame Piouk. (Enter Mme. Piouk, in great haste. Exit Jacques)
Mme. Piouk	Violette!
Mme. Krap	Marguerite! (They kiss)
Mme. Piouk	Violette!
Mme. Krap	You'll forgive me for not getting up. I have a slight pain in the—no matter. Sit down. I thought you were in Rome.
Mme. Piouk	(Sits down) How bad you look!
Mme. Krap	You're not so very blooming yourself.
Mme. Piouk	It's the traveling.
Mme. Krap	Who's this—(She looks at the card)—this Piouk?
Mme. Piouk	He's a doctor.
Mme. Krap	I'm not asking you what he does. (A knock) Come in. (Enter Marie) You may serve tea.
Marie	Very good, Madame. (She goes)
Mme. Piouk	Not for me.

Mme. Krap	Marie!
Marie	Madame?
Mme. Krap	You will serve the tea when Madame Meck is here.
Marie	Very good, Madame. (Exit)
Mme. Piouk	You're not offering me something else?
Mme. Krap	For instance?
Mme. Piouk	A glass of port.
Mme. Krap	It's time for tea.
Mme. Piouk	How is Henri?
Mme. Krap	Poorly.
Mme. Piouk	What's wrong with him?
Mme. Krap	I don't know. He no longer urinates. It's the prostate. So you got married.
Mme. Piouk	Yes.
Mme. Krap	At your age!
Mme. Piouk	We're in love.
Mme. Krap	What's the connection? (Mme. Piouk silent) But you must—I mean—you no longer must—in a word—let's see—
Mme. Piouk	Not yet.
Mme. Krap	I congratulate you.
Mme. Piouk	He wants a child.
Mme. Krap	No!
Mme. Piouk	Yes!
Mme. Krap	It's madness.
Mme. Piouk	How is Victor?

Mme. Krap	Still the same, still there, down in his hole. We never see him. (Pause) Let's not talk about it.
Mme. Piouk	You're expecting Madame Meck?
Mme. Krap	With no great impatience.
Mme. Piouk	That old witch.
Mme. Krap	You don't want to see her?
Mme. Piouk	I would just as soon not.
Mme. Krap	Yet she likes you.
Mme. Piouk	That's what you think! It's play-acting.
Mme. Krap	Yes, probably. (Pause) I expect·her any minute.
Mme. Piouk	Then I'm leaving. (She gets up)
Mme. Krap	Your husband isn't with you?
Mme. Piouk	(Sitting down again) Oh I can't wait till you see him! He's so sweet, so bright, so—
Mme. Krap	He isn't with you?
Mme. Piouk	He went to the hotel . . .
Mme. Krap	Which hotel?
Mme. Piouk	I don't know.
Mme. Krap	When will you know?
Mme. Piouk	He's supposed to pick me up here.
Mme. Krap	When?
Mme. Piouk	Oh, in about half an hour, I think.
Mme. Krap	So you can't leave.
Mme. Piouk	I would have waited for him in the drawing room.
Mme. Krap	What kind of medicine does he do?

Mme. Piouk	He doesn't have a specialty. That is—
Mme. Krap	He does everything.
Mme. Piouk	Mankind is what interests him.
Mme. Krap	Where does he perpetrate?
Mme. Piouk	He hopes to set up a practice here.
Mme. Krap	And up until now?
Mme. Piouk	Pretty much everywhere.
Mme. Krap	I haven't congratulated you. (She puts forward her cheek which Mme. Piouk kisses) You could have let me know.
Mme. Piouk	I wanted to send you a telegram but André told me that—
Mme. Krap	Anyhow all this is of no importance. (A knock) Come in. (Enter Jacques)
Jacques	Madame Meck. (Enter Mme. Meck, a bulky woman heavily laden with furs, capes, umbrella, handbag, etc. Exit Jacques)
Mme. Meck	Violette!
Mme. Krap	Jeanne! (They kiss. Mme. Meck sits down, unloads, fixes herself up) Forgive me for not getting up.
Mme. Meck	You're still in pain?
Mme. Krap	Getting worse and worse. You know my sister.
Mme. Meck	(Turning toward Mme. Piouk) Why it's Rose!
Mme. Krap	Of course not, it's Marguerite.
Mme. Meck	My dear Marguerite! (Extends her hand, which Mme. Piouk takes) Where did you come from? I thought you were in Pisa?
Mme. Krap	She's gotten married.
Mme. Meck	Married!

Mme. Krap	To a doctor who is interested in mankind.
Mme. Meck	Let me give you a kiss. (Mme. Piouk lets herself be kissed) Married! Oh!—(with an undescribable movement)—I'm so glad!
Mme. Piouk	Thank you.
Mme. Meck	What's his name?
Mme. Krap	(Looking at the card) Piouk, André.
Mme. Meck	(Ecstatically) Madame André Piouk! (A knock)
Mme. Krap	Come in. (Enter Marie with the tea tray, which she sets down on the table) Has Monsieur come back?
Marie	No, Madame.
Mme. Krap	Send Jacques in.
Marie	Very good, Madame. (Exit)
Mme. Piouk	(To Mme. Meck) Don't you find that my sister looks bad?
Mme. Meck	Bad? (Mme. Krap serves the tea, offers a cup to her sister, who refuses)
Mme. Krap	She'd rather have port.
Mme. Meck	Port! At five in the afternoon!
Mme. Krap	She's right. I'm worn out.
Mme. Piouk	What's wrong? (A knock)
Mme. Krap	Come in. (Enter Jacques) Ah, Jacques.
Jacques	Madame.
Mme. Krap	Has Monsieur come back?
Jacques	Not yet, Madame.
Mme. Krap	You will tell him, as soon as he does come back, that I have to speak to him.

Jacques	Very good, Madame.
Mme. Krap	You may turn on the light.
Jacques	Very good, Madame. (He turns on the floor lamp)
Mme. Krap	The other one too.
Jacques	Very good, Madame. (He turns on the wall lamp)
Mme. Krap	That will be all.
Jacques	Very good, Madame. (Exit)
Mme. Meck	How is he?
Mme. Krap	Who?
Mme. Meck	Henri.
Mme. Krap	Poorly.
Mme. Meck	Oh.
Mme. Krap	He doesn't piss any more.
Mme. Meck	Ooh!
Mme. Piouk	It's the prostate.
Mme. Meck	Poor thing. And he so lighthearted, so—
Mme. Krap	What's more he is eating himself up.
Mme. Piouk	For sure.
Mme. Krap	Because of Victor.
Mme. Meck	By the way, how is he?
Mme. Krap	Who?
Mme. Meck	Your Victor.
Mme. Krap	Let's not talk about it.
Mme. Meck	Me neither, I'm not doing well.

Mme. Piouk	What's the matter with you?
Mme. Meck	It's the lower belly. It's descending, so it appears.
Mme. Krap	Like me. Except that mine has descended.
Mme. Piouk	Isn't there anything to drink in this house?
Mme. Krap	To drink?
Mme. Meck	In the middle of the afternoon?
Mme. Piouk	Henri no longer pisses, Victor, we mustn't talk about it, and you, you have a descending lower belly.
Mme. Krap	And you, you've gotten married.
Mme. Meck	Is that a reason to drink?
Mme. Krap	It's of no use.
Mme. Meck	Our little Victor! What a thing to happen! And he so lighthearted, so alive!
Mme. Krap	He's never been either lighthearted or alive.
Mme. Meck	What! Why, he was the very soul of the household, for years.
Mme. Krap	The very soul of the household! Talk about something for the books.
Mme. Piouk	He's still at the Impasse de l'Enfant-Jésus?*
Mme. Krap	Jeanne sees life and lightheartedness everywhere. It's a permanent hallucination.
Mme. Piouk	He's still at the Impasse de l'Enfant-Jésus?
Mme. Krap	Still.
Mme. Piouk	He's got to be shaken up.
Mme. Krap	He doesn't get up anymore. Another cup?

---

* An alley-like street on the Left Bank, in Paris, located off the Rue de Vaugirard, between the Boulevard du Montparnasse and the Boulevard Pasteur.

Mme. Meck	Half a cup. He doesn't get up anymore, you say?
Mme. Piouk	He's ill.
Mme. Krap	Nothing at all is wrong with him.
Mme. Meck	Then why doesn't he get up anymore?
Mme. Krap	From time to time he goes out.
Mme. Meck	He gets up then from time to time.
Mme. Krap	It's when he has nothing more to eat. Then he digs around in the garbage cans. He pushes on as far as Passy*. The concierge saw him.
Mme. Meck	When you think of it, the garbage cans of Passy.
Mme. Piouk	It's horrible.
Mme. Krap	Isn't it though.
Mme. Piouk	But you do give him money?
Mme. Krap	Every month. I bring it to him myself.
Mme. Piouk	And what does he do with it?
Mme. Krap	How should I know? It's doubtless not enough. (Enter Monsieur Henri Krap)
M. Krap	Good evening, Jeanne. Well, Marguerite. (They kiss) I thought you were in Venice.
Mme. Krap	Your wife is also present. (M. Krap kisses his wife) She's gotten married.
Mme. Meck	To a doctor.
Mme. Krap	Who loves mankind.
M. Krap	(Sadly) Congratulations.

---

* A calm residential neighborhood (the sixteenth *arrondissement*).

Mme. Krap	Sit down.
M. Krap	Oh, I'm not staying.
Mme. Krap	Oh, come now, of course you are.
M. Krap	Think so? (Seats himself painfully in the armchair) I'm wrong. (Ensconces himself) I won't be able to get up again.
Mme. Krap	Don't talk nonsense.
M. Krap	My freedom is being whittled away more and more every day. Soon I won't have the right to unlock my jaw. Me, the one who expected to make an ass of himself all the way to death's door.
Mme. Meck	What's the matter with him?
Mme. Krap	He consoles himself as best he can.
M. Krap	Yes, now I've got it, now that it's too late. *Nimis sero, imber serotinus.** Peace of mind is the hallmark of slaves. (Pause. Mme. Meck making faces) I'm the cow that, up against the bars of the slaughterhouse, understands the utter absurdity of pastures. It would have done better to think about it earlier, out yonder, in the tall, tender grass. More's the pity. It still has the courtyard to cross. That nobody will be able to tear away from it.
Mme. Krap	Pay no attention. He thinks he's in his circle.
M. Krap	I am. In the ninth.† (Changing his tone) So, Marguerite, at last you're a respectable woman.
Mme. Piouk	Flatterer!
M. Krap	I'm congratulating you.
Mme. Krap	You've already congratulated her.
M. Krap	That's true.

---

* "Too late, the belated showers."

† The ninth (and lowest) circle in Dante's hell, home to its worst offenders: those treacherous to kindred, country and cause, guests, and lords and benefactors.

Mme. Piouk	Henri.
M. Krap	Yes.
Mme. Piouk	I wouldn't mind having a drink.
M. Krap	But of course. (To Mme. Krap) The bell.
Mme. Krap	You know very well I can't get up.
M. Krap	That's true. Besides it's not worth it. He'll come by himself.
Mme. Krap	Don't count on it. We've been left in peace now for three minutes.
M. Krap	So, Marguerite, if you would be good enough to ring. (Mme. Piouk gets up, rings, sits down again)
Mme. Krap	Yesterday he stayed away a good fifteen minutes before looking in. I thought he was dead. (A knock) Come in. (Enter Jacques)
M. Krap	I wonder why he always knocks. For fifteen years he's been knocking and we've been saying, Come in, and he still knocks.
Mme. Meck	It's a question of correctness.
M. Krap	(To Mme. Piouk) What will you have?
Mme. Piouk	Anything. Port.
M. Krap	(To Jacques) Port.
Jacques	Very good, sir. (Exit) (A silence)
Mme. Piouk	We were speaking about Victor.
M. Krap	Ah.
Mme. Krap	Does there exist another subject of conversation? I begin to wonder.
Mme. Meck	The poor thing!
Mme. Krap	(Violently) Be quiet!

Mme. Piouk	Violette!
Mme. Meck	What's the matter with her?
Mme. Krap	The matter is that I've had enough of hearing that scoundrel being pitied and it's been going on for two years!
Mme. Piouk	Scoundrel!
Mme. Meck	Your child!
M. Krap	Two years already! Only two!
Mme. Krap	(At the height of excitation) Let him get out of the neighborhood, the city, the county, the country, let him go croak in—in the Balkans! (A knock) As for me I—
Mme. Piouk	Come in. (Enter Jacques)
M. Krap	What do you want?
Jacques	Monsieur rang?
M. Krap	Of course not. The port.
Jacques	At once, Monsieur. (Exit) (A silence)
Mme. Meck	You were saying?
Mme. Krap	I wash my hands of it. (She gets up painfully) I've had enough. (Goes painfully to the door) Enough. (Exit)
Mme. Piouk	That's the way she can't get up.
Mme. Meck	Where is she going?
M. Krap	(With a sigh) To the toilet probably. She goes there from time to time. (A silence)
Mme. Meck	You look marvelous.
Mme. Piouk	She isn't serious.
Mme. Meck	What?

Mme. Piouk	Violette. They're idle words.
Mme. Meck	Of course. Washing her hands of him! Her only child! Can you imagine! (A knock)
M. Krap	(Too low) Come in.
Mme. Meck	A mother doing that! (Another knock)
Mme. Piouk	Come in! (Enter Jacques carrying a tray. He looks for a place to put it) Place it on the chair. (He places the tray on Mme. Krap's chair) On the other one. (He places it on the other chair) You will ask Marie to come and clear the table.
Jacques	Very good, Madame. (Exit)
Mme. Piouk	When one has servants one is no longer in one's own home.
Mme. Meck	They're needed all the same. (A silence)
Mme. Piouk	I've been without news for so long. So is there something new in this business?
M. Krap	What business?
Mme. Piouk	This business of Victor.
M. Krap	Not one new item.
Mme. Meck	It appears that he comes as far as Rue Spontini* to dig around in the garbage cans.
M. Krap	I wasn't told anything.
Mme. Piouk	You don't seem to care a bit.
M. Krap	You mean that?
Mme. Meck	I never understood a thing about this business.
M. Krap	Dramatically speaking, my wife's absence serves no purpose. (Mesdames Piouk and Meck exchange looks. A knock)

---

* A fashionable street on the Right Bank, about a mile and a half from Victor's Impasse.

Mme. Piouk	Oh, come in! (Enter Marie. Tray business. Exit Marie) Do you want some?
Mme. Meck	A drop.
Mme. Piouk	And you, Henri?
M. Krap	Thank you, no. (Mme. Piouk serves Mme. Meck)
Mme. Meck	Oh, that's too much! I'll be tipsy! (She drinks) It's strong! (Mme. Piouk serves herself, empties her glass in one gulp, pours herself a second) She's been long.
Mme. Piouk	What?
Mme. Meck	Violette has been long.
M. Krap	You think so?
Mme. Piouk	But something must be done! He can't be left like that.
M. Krap	Like what?
Mme. Piouk	In that—that sordid inertia.
M. Krap	And if it's what he wants.
Mme. Piouk	But it's a disgrace to the family!
Mme. Meck	It's not right at his age.
Mme. Piouk	It will kill Violette.
M. Krap	You don't know her. (A silence)
Mme. Piouk	(To Mme. Meck) How is the general? (A silence) Or should I say field marshal? (Handkerchief of Mme. Meck)
M. Krap	Come now, Marguerite, think about what you're saying.
Mme. Piouk	I don't understand.
M. Krap	There's a shade of difference between mourning-wear and chic.

Mme. Piouk	Oh, poor Jeanne, I didn't know, I'm dreadfully sorry, forgive me, forgive me.
Mme. Meck	(Drawing upon the military tradition) His last breath was for France. (A knock)
Mme. Piouk	That is becoming impossible.
M. Krap	We would be better off leaving the door open. Or roundly doing away with it. (Another knock)
Mme. Piouk	So just come in for crying out loud! (Enter Jacques)
Jacques	Doctor Piouk.
M. Krap	Don't know him.
Mme. Piouk	André! (Rushes out)
M. Krap	Who?
Mme. Meck	Her husband.
M. Krap	(To Jacques) Have you seen Madame?
Jacques	Madame has gone out, Monsieur.
M. Krap	Gone out!
Jacques	Yes, Monsieur.
M. Krap	On foot?
Jacques	Yes, Monsieur.
M. Krap	She didn't say where she was going?
Jacques	Madame didn't say anything, Monsieur.
M. Krap	That will do. (Exit Jacques)
Mme. Meck	Vive la France! Then came the coma.
M. Krap	I beg your pardon?
Mme. Meck	I was reliving Ludovic's last moments.

M. Krap	And then what?
Mme. Meck	Raising himself roughly into a sitting position, he cried out, Vive la France! Then he fell back and went into his death rattle.
M. Krap	He was able to raise himself into a sitting position?
Mme. Meck	Yes, to the great amazement of every one of us. (Enter Mme. and Dr. Piouk. He is a hideously ugly man. Embarrassed silence. Introductions. Dr. Piouk sits down)
Mme. Piouk	A bit of port, my darling?
Dr. Piouk	Thank you.
Mme. Piouk	Thank you yes or no thank you?
Dr. Piouk	No thank you.
M. Krap	You'll excuse me for not getting up. I have a slight pain in the—I'm tired.
Dr. Piouk	You are suffering?
M. Krap	Dying.
Mme. Meck	Come, come, Henri, calm down.
M. Krap	And I have every intention of amazing nobody.
Mme. Meck	Henri!
M. Krap	By raising myself into a sitting position.
Mme. Piouk	Where is Violette?
M. Krap	My unbefitting position. Ha! Ha!
Dr. Piouk	A little port, after all. (Mme. Piouk serves him)
Mme. Meck	She went out.
M. Krap	What?
Mme. Meck	Marguerite is asking where Violette is. I am telling her she went out.

Mme. Piouk	(Decanter in hand) Went out!
M. Krap	On foot.
Mme. Meck	Without saying where she was going.
M. Krap	She won't be long getting back.
Mme. Piouk	She told you?
M. Krap	She's never long getting back.
Mme. Meck	May what you say be the truth.
M. Krap	Why?
Mme. Meck	I'll be able to leave with an easy mind.
M. Krap	My son's way is the truth.
Mme. Piouk	Henri!
M. Krap	I'm cutting loose.
Mme. Meck	(Pursuing her train of thought) Without seeing her in my mind's eye, all bloody, run over by a truck.
M. Krap	It's she who runs over the trucks.
Dr. Piouk	(Getting up) My darling—
M. Krap	My darling, my darling.
Dr. Piouk	It is time we left.
M. Krap	Jeanne.
Mme. Meck	Henri.
M. Krap	You remember the early days of my marriage to Violette?
Mme. Meck	Do I remember!
M. Krap	Before we'd learned to appreciate each other. Those were the good old days. Did I have occasion to say darling to her?

Mme. Meck	You used to coo.
M. Krap	I can't imagine.
Dr. Piouk	(Still standing) Marguerite.
Mme. Piouk	I'm coming, darling.
M. Krap	My wife will be so sorry. Terribly so.
Mme. Meck	Me too, I should also be going.
M. Krap	But you're staying.
Mme. Meck	That is—
M. Krap	You see, the world outside is calling to her, but she makes a point of holding out. But Marguerite has never been led by anything but her own inclinations. I'm not saying this for your benefit, Doctor.
Mme. Piouk	You're being ungracious, Henri.
M. Krap	(Without warmth) Stay for dinner, we're having cold cuts.
Dr. Piouk	Most kind. Unfortunately we are expected elsewhere.
M. Krap	(To Mme. Meck, lewdly) Aren't they in a hurry!
Mme. Meck	Be patient just five more minutes.
M. Krap	Come, come, a little restraint.
Mme. Meck	I will bring you back. In the Delage.*
Dr. Piouk	How about it, Marguerite?
Mme. Piouk	Whatever you like, my darling.
M. Krap	The longer you wait, the better it is.
Mme. Piouk	I would so have liked you—Violette to get to know you. (Dr. Piouk sits down again. A silence)

---

* A luxury car named after Louis Delage, French industrialist and engineer.

M. Krap	Vous prenez un cigare?
Dr. Piouk	Thank you.
M. Krap	Thank you yes or no thank you?
Dr. Piouk	I don't smoke. (A silence)
Mme. Meck Mme. Piouk	(Together) I—
Mme. Meck	Oh, sorry. You were saying?
Mme. Piouk	Oh, nothing. Go on. (A silence)
M. Krap	Well, Jeanne, spit it out.
Mme. Meck	(Upon reflection) My goodness, I don't know any more. (A silence)
M. Krap	Incapable of reflection myself, it is my organs that have taken over. (A silence) It is with you, Doctor, that I am striving to open communication.
Dr. Piouk	Oh, you know, I'm not much of a talker.
Mme. Piouk	He thinks so much!
M. Krap	Nonetheless, what I've just said isn't devoid of intelligence.
Dr. Piouk	It is meaningless.
M. Krap	Wait a minute! Meaning what?
Dr. Piouk	You are your organs, Monsieur, and your organs are you.
M. Krap	I am my organs?
Dr. Piouk	That is so.
M. Krap	You are frightening me.
Mme. Meck	(Sniffing out free medical advice) And me, Doctor, am I also my organs?
Dr. Piouk	Without the least bit left over, Madame.

M. Krap	What a pleasure to meet at last an intelligent man!
Mme. Piouk	(Ecstatically) André!
M. Krap	Please do go on. Elaborate on this grandiose train of thought.
Dr. Piouk	This isn't the right time.
M. Krap	Before the return of that heap of obsolete organs known as my wife.
Mme. Piouk	Henri!
Dr. Piouk	Please.
M. Krap	You're going to force me to visit your office. (A knock)
Mme. Piouk	Come in. (Enter Jacques)
Jacques	Mademoiselle Skunk. (Enter Mademoiselle Skunk, an alluring young lady. Greetings, hers glum. Exit Jacques)
Mme. Piouk	You remember me?
Mlle. Skunk	Of course.
Mme. Piouk	It was two years ago, at Evian.
Mlle. Skunk	What was I doing there? (A silence)
Mme. Piouk	May I introduce you to my husband, Doctor Piouk. (Mlle. Skunk sits down in Mme. Krap's seat)
Mme. Meck	You look marvelous.
Mme. Piouk	A bit of port?
Mlle. Skunk	If you like.
M. Krap	Doctor.
Dr. Piouk	(Torn from his thoughts, makes a show of giving a start) Did someone call my name?
M. Krap	I'm wondering of what use you're going to be in this farce.

Dr. Piouk	(Upon mature reflection) I hope that I will be able to be useful.
Mme. Meck	(Worried) I don't understand.
Dr. Piouk	And your role, my dear sir, is it very clear-cut?
M. Krap	It is being cut.
Dr. Piouk	Yet you are on stage.
M. Krap	So it appears.
Mme. Meck	I absolutely must go.
M. Krap	Go, my dear Jeanne, go, since go you absolutely must. We don't need you.
Mlle. Skunk	Where is Violette?
Dr. Piouk	(To M. Krap) Forcing things a bit you might perhaps manage to amuse the rubbernecks.
M. Krap	You think so? From the bottom of your heart?
Dr. Piouk	I say it as I think it.
M. Krap	That is a possibility I hadn't caught sight of.
Mlle. Skunk	Where is Violette?
Mme. Meck	It is getting worrisome.
M. Krap	What are you saying?
Mme. Meck	Olga is asking where Violette is and I am saying it is getting worrisome.
M. Krap	What is getting worrisome?
Mme. Meck	This inordinate absence.
M. Krap	Inordinate absence! Only Jeanne comes up with words like that.
Mlle. Skunk	Where did she go?

Mme. Meck	That we do not know.
M. Krap	Driven by who knows what she left the house on a sudden impulse, on foot. For the longest time we thought she was in the toilet. That's it, right, Doctor?
Dr. Piouk	Intricate to a fault. Keep at it.
Mlle. Skunk	She asked me to come by before dinner.
M. Krap	She had to speak to you?
Mlle. Skunk	Yes, about things that couldn't wait.
M. Krap	She had to speak to me as well, so it appears. In fact it is the only reason why I am here among you, as you can easily imagine. And yet she still hasn't told me anything.
Mme. Meck	(To Mlle. Skunk) Have you seen Victor?
M. Krap	Right now I'm the one who goes to speak to him.
Mlle. Skunk	Last week.
M. Krap	(To Dr. Piouk) Mlle. Skunk is my son's fiancée.
Dr. Piouk	Fortunate young man.
Mlle. Skunk	(Bitterly) He cannot contain himself for joy. (Dr. Piouk lights a cigarette)
M. Krap	I thought you didn't smoke.
Dr. Piouk	I lied to you.
Mme. Meck	I am going to have to leave.
M. Krap	You're not going to start in again.
Mme. Meck	What's to be done?
M. Krap	The time one wastes with such people. Go. We will call you.
Mlle. Skunk	I am going with you. (A fierce-sounding voice is heard)
M. Krap	Peekaboo, there she is.

Mme. Meck	At last!
Dr. Piouk	(To Mlle. Skunk) You're French, Mademoiselle?
Mlle. Skunk	No, Monsieur.
Mme. Meck	You are sure that it's her?
M. Krap	I am convinced of it.
Dr. Piouk	Scandinavian? (A knock)
Mme. Piouk	Come in. (Enter Jacques)
Jacques	Madame is asking for Monsieur.
M. Krap	It sounds like a classified ad.
Mme. Meck	There isn't anything the matter with Madame?
M. Krap	You will tell Madame that—(Changes his mind). Help resuscitate me. (Jacques rushes over, helps M. Krap to get up, wants to hold him up as far as the door. M. Krap motions to him to get out of the way. Reaching the door he turns around) You see! Once I'm up I walk all by myself. I go out! (Exit. He comes back in) I come back in! And I go back out! (Exit, followed by Jacques)
Mme. Piouk	Henri is very much changed.
Dr. Piouk	Don't tell me you are English.
Mme. Meck	Believing he is doomed, he no longer restrains himself.
Mme. Piouk	That's convenient.
Dr. Piouk	(Disheartened) He's a remarkable man.
Mme. Piouk	You really think so?
Dr. Piouk	I say it as I think it.
Mme. Piouk	But from what viewpoint?
Dr. Piouk	That is difficult to say.

Mme. Piouk	Indeed this is the first time I am hearing it.
Dr. Piouk	What does he do?
Mme. Meck	(With pride) He is a man of letters.
Dr. Piouk	You don't say! (Enter M. Krap. He reaches his armchair and cautiously sits down)
M. Krap	You were saying nice things about me, I feel it.
Mme. Meck	There isn't anything the matter with her?
M. Krap	She is unharmed.
Mme. Meck	She is coming?
M. Krap	She's getting ready for that.
Mme. Piouk	There was a time when you were unaffected.
M. Krap	At the cost of what artifice!
Dr. Piouk	You are a writer, Monsieur?
M. Krap	(Indignant) What gives you leave to—
Dr. Piouk	It can be felt in the way you express yourself.
Mme. Piouk	Where has she been?
Mme. Meck	She is going to tell us.
M. Krap	I will be frank with you. I was a writer.
Mme. Meck	He is a member of the Institute!
M. Krap	What did I tell you.
Dr. Piouk	What genre?
M. Krap	I don't follow you.
Dr. Piouk	I speak of your writings. Your preferences were for what genre?
M. Krap	For the shit genre.

Mme. Piouk	Really.
⁓ ⁔uk	Prose or poetry?
M. Krap	One day the former, another day the latter.
Dr. Piouk	And you now deem your body of work to be complete?
M. Krap	The Lord has flushed me out.
Dr. Piouk	A small book of memoirs does not tempt you?
M. Krap	That would spoil the death throes.
Mme. Meck	Admit that this is a bizarre way to treat one's guests.
Mlle. Skunk	Extremely odd.
M. Krap	Marguerite, would you mind changing places with Olga?
Mme. Piouk	I am happy where I am.
M. Krap	I know. We are all happy where we are. Very, very happy. Unfortunately our happiness is not the issue.
Mme. Meck	Which new freak is this?
M. Krap	Don't you see, Marguerite, since you do need to be told everything, whether we see you or whether we don't see you is so to speak of no importance. I for one would not see the slightest drawback in your disappearing this very minute. Olga, on the other hand, has a place among us only insofar as she shows off her charms, that is to say her breasts and her legs, for her face is rather commonplace.
Mme. Piouk	As a boor you are moving ahead.
M. Krap	Marguerite, you are wrong to take offense. As a brother-in-law I'm fond of you, very fond, and I would be absolutely heartbroken to see you move away. But as a—how can I put it—(He snaps his fingers)
Dr. Piouk	Hierophant.
M. Krap	If you like. (A silence)

Dr. Piouk	So, finish your phrase.
M. Krap	What was I saying?
Dr. Piouk	As a brother-in-law you are fond of her, as a hierophant you—?
M. Krap	(His voice breaking) I have no family.
Mme. Piouk	He is crying!
Dr. Piouk	Do as he asks, Marguerite. (Mme. Piouk and Mlle. Skunk change places)
M. Krap	(To Mlle. Skunk) Open up your jacket. Cross your legs. Lift your skirt. (He helps her) There. Don't budge one inch. This is what we call a momentary lapse. I am subject to a fair number of them.
Mme. Meck	(Exploding) I have had enough!
M. Krap	We have all had enough. But that is not the issue.
Mme. Meck	For me it is the issue. (Rises massively and gathers her numerous belongings. Digs around in her enormous bag, finally brings out a card and reads) *I must see you. Come have tea tomorrow. I have a million things to tell you. We will be alone.* (She allows time for the message to have its effect) I don't like to have my leg pulled.
M. Krap	People are truly unbelievable.
Dr. Piouk	It is human nature.
M. Krap	The minute they believe they are not having their leg pulled, they put up with everything.
Dr. Piouk	We are put together just that way.
M. Krap	Poor Jeanne, you might just as well stay seated as beat around the bush standing up, giving way under the weight of your equipment. She commands the stage, by God, and it hasn't got a thing to do with her!

Mme. Meck	(In the tone of a pythoness) I am but an old woman, ugly, ill and alone. Yet the day will come when all of you envy me. (A silence)
M. Krap	Touché. (Exit Mme. Meck, slamming the door)
Dr. Piouk	She has great foresight.
M. Krap	But whom don't we envy?
Dr. Piouk	She perhaps has a function you don't suspect.
M. Krap	Doctor, you are getting caught up in the game! Watch out!
Dr. Piouk	I won't deny its charm.
Mlle. Skunk	(Yawning deeply) Sorry!
Mme. Piouk	But this light is horrible!
Mlle. Skunk	You are no longer under it though.
Mme. Piouk	Now I see it.
Mlle. Skunk	What is this wire for? (She points to a thin strip of barbed wire which, held in place beneath the edge of the table, extends down to the floor)
Mme. Piouk	Wire?
Mlle. Skunk	(Putting her hand on it) It has sharp points! Look.(Mme. Piouk gets up and leans forward over the table)
Mme. Piouk	How is it that I didn't notice it?
Dr. Piouk	My wife is but barely attuned to the macrocosm.
M. Krap	Yet she did react to the lighting.
Dr. Piouk	It's that it really made her suffer.
Mlle. Skunk	But what is the meaning of that?
M. Krap	It is Victor's seat.
Dr. Piouk	He is your son?

M. Krap	Yes, I am sure of it now.
Dr. Piouk	He took up a lot of space?
M. Krap	Yes, he took hold of a lot of space, in this house.
Mlle. Skunk	I don't understand.
M. Krap	What don't you understand, my little Olga?
Mlle. Skunk	What that (She points to the wire) has to do with Victor.
M. Krap	Everything has to be explained to them.
Dr. Piouk	There you have woman.
M. Krap	Don't you see, my little Olga, since Victor's departure, about two years ago, I believe—
Mlle. Skunk	Two years! Two years five months!
M. Krap	What is important about that?
Mlle. Skunk	For heaven's sake!
M. Krap	Shall I go on? (A silence) Since that—er—that event, my wife has always had the desire to preserve, while so to speak doing away with, the spots favored by our son, for all of us had our favorite spots in this house, Victor, my wife, and I, going as far back as I can remember, and speaking for myself personally I am still holding on to mine. (Pause) My wife threw herself into this project—long postponed, why I don't know—last week, and the results lie here before you. And it is only a beginning. Soon the apartment will be full of barbed wire. (Pause) It must be said, in Violette's defense, that for one whole afternoon she was under the spell of the Surrealist Exhibition. (Pause) Is this sufficiently clear?
Dr. Piouk	Much too clear. You have botched everything.
M. Krap	Doctor, you disappoint me.
Dr. Piouk	Are you insinuating that I've said something stupid?

Mme. Piouk	He is insane.
M. Krap	Immensely stupid, Doctor. For one must smile at one's own smile.
Dr. Piouk	You are right, Marguerite. (Enter Mme. Krap)
M. Krap	Enter the Rock of Gibraltar.
Mme. Piouk	André, this is my sister. Violette, I— (Dr. Piouk gets up)
M. Krap	I am sorry for not getting up. I have a slight pain in the—
Mme. Krap	Marguerite, you have taken my seat.
Mme. Piouk	(Rising hastily) Take it. (Mme. Krap sits down in her seat, Mme. Piouk sits down in that of Mme. Meck)
Mme. Krap	Good evening, Olga.
Mlle. Skunk	Good evening. You wanted to see me?
Mme. Krap	Yes. Who is this man?
Mme. Piouk	He is my husband. (She gets up) Coming, André?
Mme. Krap	(Forcefully) Sit down! (Mme. Piouk wavers)
M. Krap	Be careful. (Mme. Piouk sits down again)
Mme. Krap	Doctor—let's see—
Dr. Piouk	Piouk. (He bows and sits down again)
Mme. Krap	Marguerite has told us that you love mankind. Is that possible?
Mme. Piouk	You distort my words.
Dr. Piouk	I do not love it.
Mme. Piouk	It interests him. Period.
Mme. Krap	You are interested in mankind?
Dr. Piouk	It has its moments.

Mme. Krap   You are not a Communist?

Dr. Piouk   My private life is my own business.

M. Krap   Doctor, don't make things worse.

Mme. Piouk   Where have you been? We were beginning to worry. André did not want to wait. But when I told him how much you wanted to meet him—

Mme. Krap   It is a sticky problem.

Dr. Piouk   Which one?

Mme. Krap   That of mankind.

Dr. Piouk   Offhand, I would agree.

M. Krap   The best thinkers have wrestled with it.

Dr. Piouk   I do not pretend to have surpassed them.

Mme. Krap   And what is your solution?

Dr. Piouk   My solution?

M. Krap   In a word.

Mme. Krap   (Sternly) You do have one, I hope.

Dr. Piouk   It lacks charm.

M. Krap   That can't be helped.

Dr. Piouk   Is this really the right time?

M. Krap   It is certainly the first time I have heard someone being pleaded with—

Mme. Krap   Be quiet!

M. Krap   To clear up the situation of the human race.

Dr. Piouk   It does not seem to be the right moment.

Mme. Krap   We will be the judge of that.

M. Krap	Do your duty.
Dr. Piouk	So, here is what I would do—
M. Krap	There are things to do?
Dr. Piouk	I am a practical soul.
Mme. Krap	Would you be quiet?
M. Krap	Yes, Violette, I would indeed.
Mme. Krap	We are listening.

Dr. Piouk: Here it is. I would prohibit reproduction. I would perfect the condom and other appliances and generalize their use. I would create a state-run corps of abortionists. I would impose the death sentence on every woman guilty of having given birth. I would drown the newborn. I would campaign in favor of homosexuality and myself set the example. And to get things going, I would encourage by every means the recourse to euthanasia, without, however, making it an obligation. Here you have the broad outlines.

Mme. Krap: I was born too soon.

M. Krap: Much too soon.

Dr. Piouk: I do not lay claim to originality. It is a matter of organization. There is where I have opened up new horizons. In two years everything will be in position. Unfortunately, my strength is ebbing. My inner resources as well.

Mme. Krap: And that child you want?

Dr. Piouk: Who told you that I want a child? (A silence)

Mme. Piouk: (To Mme. Krap) You are hateful.

Mme. Krap: Doctor, you will kill her.

Dr. Piouk: I want a child, first off, to amuse me during my leisure hours, more and more brief and dreary; second, that it should receive the torch from my hands, when they can no longer bear it.

M. Krap	That in essence is the advantage of sons.
Mme. Krap	But you will kill her.
Dr. Piouk	For a long time I have been debating this very question with your sister, Madame, quite as much before as since we were united. Isn't that so, Marguerite?
Mme. Piouk	You were just perfect.
Dr. Piouk	During those delightful, awful weeks preceding our vows, while we roamed hand in hand in the Campagna or, on the terraces of Tivoli, sought the advice of the moon, our conversation ran almost entirely on this very question. Isn't that so, Marguerite?
Mme. Piouk	Almost solely, my darling.
Mme. Krap	(To M. Krap) What's the matter with you, there, sneering away in your corner?
M. Krap	I was thinking about the moon and you and me, seeking its advice.
Dr. Piouk	Engaged at last, we went through hideous periods and, speaking for myself, I would not want to relive them, not for anything.
M. Krap	What can you do? Engaged humans are that way. I recall a certain night, in Robinson.* Violette was ahead of me in the tree and I assure you—
Mme. Krap	Be quiet!
Dr. Piouk	And since our official, open cohabitation which, by the way, was blessed by His Holiness, how many nights have we not worn out, until cockcrow, weighing the pros and cons, incapable of making a decision?
M. Krap	You should have taken the plunge head first.

---

* Plessis-Robinson, a suburban center southwest of Paris.

Dr. Piouk	That is what we did— (He takes out his memorandum book and flips through it) —wait—on the Saturday night preceding Sunday last. (He turns a few pages, makes a note of something, puts the memorandum book back in his pocket) And you see, we were sick and tired of splitting hairs. (Expressive gesture) Now we are waiting. (He gets up) And by the will of God.
Mme. Krap	What is the matter with you?
Dr. Piouk	The matter with me?
Mme. Krap	You are not going to leave us?
M. Krap	I invited them for dinner. But they are all fired up to be alone.
Mme. Krap	To stay for dinner! Using what?
M. Krap	I don't know. Yesterday's lamb.
Mme. Krap	Lamb! You mean mutton. What am I saying, mutton, ram, it smells of wool and coupling all over the house.
Dr. Piouk	You tempt me. Unfortunately we are expected somewhere.
M. Krap	Put yourself in their place.
Mme. Krap	If I were fifty, no, that's too much, forty years younger, Doctor, I would go with you to all the hot spots, in spite of the fact that strictly speaking you do not make much of an impression on me. But when you speak . . . ! (To M. Krap) What are you saying?
M. Krap	Nothing. I was quivering.
Mme. Piouk	We are expected somewhere.
Dr. Piouk	Now let's not get carried away, dearest.
Mme. Krap	Let's go to the Terminus.
Dr. Piouk	Mlle. Skunk is not saying anything.
Mlle. Skunk	What do you want me to say? I am waiting to know why I was summoned.

Mme. Krap	You will come with us. We'll all get drunk.
Dr. Piouk	I just love blowouts.
M. Krap	And your lower belly?
Mme. Krap	I will speak to the Doctor about it. Would you be so kind, Doctor?
Dr. Piouk	Not before the cheese, dear lady.
Mme. Krap	Look here, you rascal you!
Mme. Piouk	(To Mme. Krap) Your outing did you a world of good. (A silence)
Dr. Piouk	You will come, Mademoiselle?
Mlle. Skunk	I am free.
Mme. Krap	It's decided. The Terminus, in half an hour.

Translated from the French by Michael Brodsky

Afterword

Explicating Beckett, for yourself, let alone others, is akin to putting a Slinky toy on the floor, contracting and expanding it, placing mirrors at all angles to it, photographing it, then reviewing the mystifying, haunting negative.

For me, reading *Eleuthéria*, hearing it, seeing it, releases all the concealed Beckettian concatenations. Therein is the unnervingly familiar feeling of looking through Hamm and Clov's telescope the wrong way. There is nothing *out* there, but there is certainly something *inside*, an interior world of intertwining figures, motifs, and dreams.

I have always felt, very personally, that the most poignant of all of Beckett's writing appears in *Krapp's Last Tape*—in particular when Krapp says:

> I lay down across her with my face in her breasts and my hand on her. We lay there without moving. But under us all moved, and moved us, gently, up and down, and from side to side.

In *Eleuthéria*, we find M. Krap saying to his wife:

M. Krap   (Animatedly) That is it! That is it! Let's keep it since it is here! (Pause) We were on the water. Your oarsman had a knife. I was no longer rowing. The waves rocked us. (Pause) He too was rocked by the waves. (Pause) You are sure that he is mine?

Mme. Krap   (Upon reflection) There is—er—a seventy percent chance.

M. Krap   My stock is rising.

Mme. Krap   That is all?

M. Krap   Ah yes, that is all.

A beautiful tiger chasing its elusive tail: It is the Beckett continuum, the wild humor and truth and sadness. In *Endgame*, Clov refuses the forlorn Hamm's request for a parting kiss; in *Eleuthéria*, the beautiful Olga Skunk cannot bring herself to kiss the dying M. Krap, nor can his wife. "Oh, not now Henri, I am so late," she complains. "That is true," he says.

In another passage, evocative of *Waiting for Godot*, Mme. Krap asks, "What am I going to do?":

M. Krap   You are not going over there anymore?

Mme. Krap   I don't know.

M. Krap   But you have no more tricks up your sleeve. (An interval) Unless you find something else.

Mme. Krap   For sure we will find something. It cannot go on like this.

M. Krap   Bravo!

Mme. Krap   Can it?

M. Krap   Why, of course not. For sure we will find something. (Mme. Krap gets up) So that it does go on like this.

Mme. Krap   What?

When John Oakes, Dan Simon, and I undertook to publish the Greek-titled *Eleuthéria*, we launched ourselves on our own Odyssean voyage. Passing through and around various perils and problems, we are now able to deliver it to our symbolic Penelope. And here is her gift, *eleuthéria (freedom)*, finally moored in its proper port.

—Barney Rosset, April 1995.

Coprophilus

—after Martial

a poet whose talent is
as small as his minus-

cule mentula has been
slandering me in the

taverns alleging that
my verses are stolen

from those of my friend
Catullus   He misses the

mark   I simply ridicule
the opinions of a man

(if he is a man) who
can only ejaculate if

he has dined on his
own foul excrement.

The African Negro Art Exhibition

Museum of Modern Art, 1935

In 1935, the Museum of Modern Art in New York commissioned Walker Evans to document *African Negro Art*, an exhibition directed by James Johnson Sweeney. The show was intended to increase awareness of African art and to demonstrate its influence on contemporary European and American artists. Evans was asked to produce a photographic record of the exhibition that would travel to universities as a teaching tool. These documents, tightly framed and uniformly lit, are today recognized as powerful works of art themselves.

Unidentified.
p. 117

Mask. Cameroon. Wood decorated with red seeds,
12 ½ inches high. Collection Pierre Loeb, Paris.
p. 118

Mask. Cameroon. Wood, 18 ⅛ inches high. Collection Museum für
Völkerkunde, Leipzig. Headdress shows animal motive (spider?).
p. 119

Mask. Ivory Coast. Wood, 13 inches high.
Collection André Lhote, Paris.
p. 120

Mask representing an animal. French Sudan. Polychrome wood,
17 ¾ inches high. Collection Musée d'Ethnographie, Palais du
Trocadéro, Paris. Used in funerary or commemorative rites.
p. 121

Janus head. Cross River, Cameroon. Parchment stretched over wood,
9 ⅞ inches high. Collection Antony Moris, Paris. Represents male and female
elements in the universe. Used in war dances, possibly carried on pole.
This photograph shows a view of one face.
p. 122

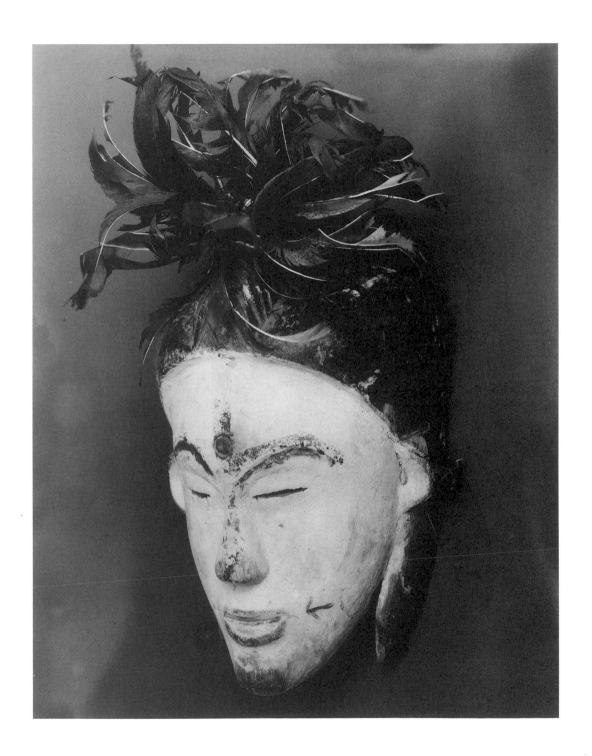

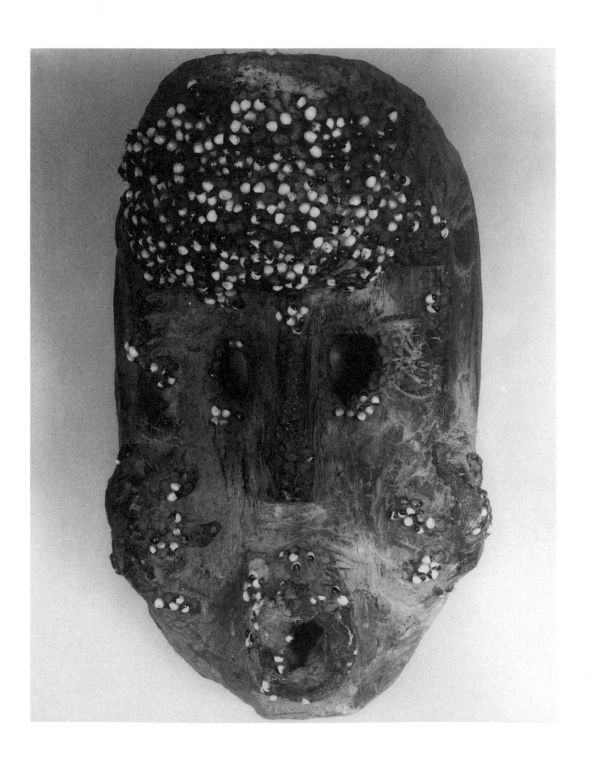

118

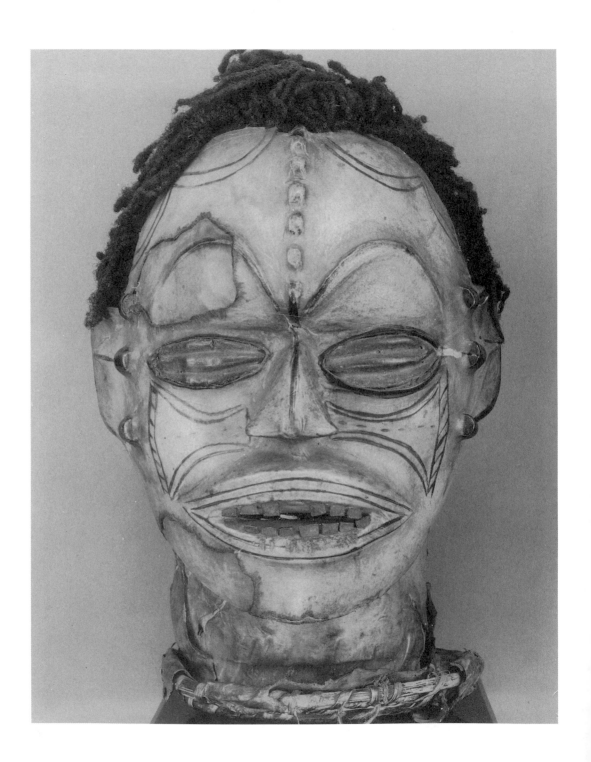

Chapter and Verse

They were ushered along to the water's edge
to wait. Then one further back on the bank
said drink, so they drank, some of them
cupping their hands, taking the water like gods,
and some of them kneeling and lapping the water
like dogs.

And those that had sunk to their knees, gone down
on all fours, they were taken aside and tried
for stooping as low as a beast, but moreover
for kissing themselves on the lips in the lake.
They were all of them guilty and gathered together
and thumped. In the face. And those that were saved
were rewarded with mirrors and cups and praise
having made at the lake such a lasting impression.

Here endeth the first lesson.

A Week and a Fortnight

Tricked into life with a needle and knife
but marked with the cross in the eye of a rifle,
laid from the first in the grave of a cradle.

Fed with the flesh not the fur of a peach
but bruised in the garden, tripped in the street,
bunged with a bottle of petrol and bleach.

Nursed at the breast on the cream of the nipple
but branded for keeps with the print of a fist,
buffed with a handkerchief, flannelled with spittle.

Baubled and bangled from ankle to wrist
but milked for a season, stung by a cousin,
dunked for a bet on the hob of an oven.

Picked for a prize for the fair of his face
but kicked to the foot from the head of the stairs,
buckled and belted and leathered and laced.

Spared from a stunt in the mouth of a lion
but dabbed on the foot with a soldering iron,
stabbed in the palm with a smoldering stub.

Left for an hour with booze and a razor
but carted by ambulance clear of the woods,
saved at last by drugs and a laser.

Days for the dirty, life for the lost,
the acts of mercy and the stations of the cross,
the seven acts of mercy and the fourteen stations of the cross.

A Basket Full of Wallpaper

Some people said that he'd been a chicken-sexer during the Forties, a pale and narrow man who had spent his days interned in a camp for the Japanese near the mountains of Idaho. Endless months spent determining whether chickens were male or female. He had come to Ireland to forget it all. At other times, the older men, elbows on the bar counter, invented heinous crimes for him. In Japan, they said, he had attached electrical cords to the testicles of airmen, ritually sliced prisoners with swords, operated slow drip torture on young Marines. They said he had that sort of face. Dark eyes falling down into sunken cheeks, a full mouth without any color, a tiny scar over his right eye. Even the women created a fantastic history for him. He was the fourth son of an emperor, or a poet, or a general, carrying the baggage of unrequited love. To us boys at school he was a kamikaze pilot who had gotten cold feet, barreling out in a parachute and somehow drifting to our town, carried by some ferocious, magical wave.

On the beach he walked with his head slung low to the ground, stooping to collect stones. We would sometimes hide in the dunes, parting the long grass to watch him, his trouser pockets filling up with stones. He had a long rambling stride, sometimes walking for hours along the coast, the gulls hurling themselves up from the strand, small fishing boats bobbing on the sea. When I was twelve years old I saw him leap along the beach while a porpoise surfaced and resurfaced in the water, fifty yards away. Once Paul Ryan wrapped a note around a brick and flung it through the window of his cottage, one of a row of fifteen small houses in the center of our village. *Nip go home*, said the note. The following day we noticed that the window had been covered with wallpaper and Paul Ryan went home from school with blood caked under his nose because we could no longer see through Osobe's front window.

Osobe had come to Ireland before I was born, some time in the Fifties. He would have been a curious sight in any Irish town, his black hair sticking out like conifer needles, his eyes shaded by the brim of his brown hat. He had bought the cottage, a dilapidated two-room affair, from an out-of-town landlord who thought that Osobe might stay for just a month or two. But, according to my father, a huge lorry carrying reams and reams of wallpaper pulled up to the cottage during the first summer of his visit. Osobe and two hefty Dubliners lifted all the paper into the house and later he hung a sign on his front window: *Wallpaper for Sale—Ask Inside*. There were mutterings about how the paper had been stolen, how it had been imported from Japan at a ridiculous price, undercutting the Irish wholesalers. Nobody bought any for a month until my Aunt Moira, who was infamous for having gotten drunk with Brendan Behan in a Republican pub in Dublin, knocked on his door and ordered a floral pattern with a touch of pink for her living room.

Osobe rode his black bicycle along the river out to her house. Rolls of paper, cans of glue, knives, and brushes were stuffed into the basket. My aunt said he did a wonderful job, although people muttered about her outside mass on Sunday mornings. "He was as quiet then as he is now," she told me. "No more noise out of him than a dormouse and we should leave it that way. He's a good man who never done anyone a whit of harm." She laughed at the rumors that hung around him.

By the time I was born he was a fixture around town, no stranger than the newspaper editor whose handkerchiefs drooped from his trouser pockets, the shopkeeper who stole all the footballs that landed in her back garden, the soldier who had lost his right hand fighting for Franco. People nodded to him on the streets and, in Gaffney's pub, he was left alone over his morning pint of Guinness. He had a brisk trade going with the wallpaper and occasionally when Kieran O'Malley, the local handyman, was sick, he was called out to unblock a toilet or fix a crooked door. There was talk that he was seeing a young girl from Galway, a madwoman who walked around with three sleeves sewn on her dresses. But that had about as much truth as all the other rumors—or less, in fact, since he was never seen to leave town, not even on his bicycle.

He spoke English only haltingly and in the shops he would whisper for a packet of cigarettes or a jar of jam. On Sundays he never wore his brown hat. Girls giggled when he passed them in the street, a red Japanese sun umbrella held above his head. I was sixteen years old when he hung a sign on his front door, looking for help with a wallpaper job. It was a hot summer, the ground was bone dry, and there were no seasonal jobs in the fields. My father would moan at the dinner table about the huge toll that emigration was having on his undertaking business. "Everyone's gone somewhere else to die," he'd say. "Even that bloody Mrs. Hynes is hanging on for dear life." One evening my mother came and sat by my bed, mashing her fingers together nervously. She muttered under her breath that I should get some work with the Japanese man, that I was old enough now to put some bread on the table. I had noticed that, in the bread that she baked at home, there were no currants anymore.

The following morning, in a blue wool jumper and old working trousers, I sidled down to his house and knocked on his door.

The cottage was filled with rolls of wallpaper. They were stacked on top of each other all around the room, crowding in toward the small table and two wooden chairs. Most of it was muted in color, but together they made a strange collage, flowers and vines and odd shapes all meshed together. The walls themselves had been papered with dozens of different types and the smell of paste was heavy in the house. On the ground sat rows and rows of small paper dolls, the faces painted almost comically. An old philosopher, a young girl, a wizened woman, a soldier. A row of Japanese books lay in one corner. On top of them, a pan of sliced bread. Cigarette packages littered the floor. There was a collection of beach stones on the mantelpiece. I noticed lots of change, a few pound notes scattered around the cottage, and a twenty-pound note stuffed under a lamp. A kettle whistled on the stove and he filled up two china cups with tea.

"Welcome," he said. The saucer rattled in my fingers. "There is big job in house. You will help me?"

I nodded and sipped at the tea, which tasted peculiarly bitter.

His hands were long and spindly. I noticed the liver spots gathering up from his wrists. A gray shirt slouched on his thin shoulders.

"You will go home and get bicycle, in this afternoon we start. Very good?"

We rode out together to the old Gorman house, which had lain empty for three years. Osobe whistled as we pedaled and people stared at us from their cars and houses. Five rolls of pale green wallpaper were balanced in his front basket and I carried two cans of paste in my right hand, steering the bicycle with the other. I saw Paul Ryan hanging out by the school, smoking a long cigar. "Ya get slanty eyes from wanking too much, Donnelly," he shouted, and I tucked my head down toward the handlebars.

The Gorman House had been bought by an American millionaire just three months before. There were schoolboy rumors that the American drove a huge Cadillac and had five blonde daughters who would be fond of the local disco and, on excellent authority, were known to romp behind haystacks. But there was nobody there when we arrived on our bicycles. Osobe produced a set of keys from his overalls and walked slowly through the house, pointing at the walls, motes of dust kicking up from behind him. We made five trips on the bikes that day, carrying reams of wallpaper and paste each time. At the end of the day, after I had carried a ladder over my shoulder from his house, he produced a brand new ten-pound note and offered it to me.

"Tomorrow we start," he said, and then he bowed slightly. "You are fast on bicycle," he said.

I went outside. The sun was slouching over the town. I heard Osobe humming in the background as I leaped on my bike and rode toward home, the money stuffed down deep in my pocket.

That summer I read books in my bedroom and I wanted Osobe to tell me a fabulous story about his past. I suppose I wanted to own something of him, to make his history belong to me.

It would have something to do with Hiroshima, I had decided, with the children of the pikadon, the flash boom. There would be charred telegraph poles and tree trunks, a wasteland of concrete, a single remaining shell of a building. People with melted faces would run wildly through the streets. Bloated corpses would float down the Ota River. The slates on the roofs of houses would bubble. He would spit on the American and British soldiers as they sat under burnt cherry blossom trees, working the chewing gum over in their mouths. Perhaps, in his story, he would reach out for the festered face of a young girl. Or massage the burnt scalp of a boy. A woman friend of his would see her reflection in a bowl of soup and howl. Maybe he would run off toward the hills and never stop. Or perhaps he would simply just walk away, down narrow roads, in wooden sandals, a begging bowl in his hands. It would be a peculiar Buddhist hell, that story of his, and a B-29 would drone in constantly from the clouds.

But Osobe stayed silent almost all the time as he stood in that big old house and rolled paste on the walls in long smooth motions, humming gently as the house began to take on color. "Sean," he would say to me in comically broken English, with his face cocked into a smile, "some day you will be great wallpaper man. You must think how important this job. We make people happy, or sad if we do bad job."

He would buy big bottles of Club Orange and packets of Gold-grain biscuits, and spread them out on the ground during lunchtime. He brought a radio one morning and his old body swayed with laughter as he tuned in to a pop station from Dublin. Once, for a joke, he swiped a ladder away from me and left me hanging from a ledge. He was deft with a knife, slicing the wallpaper in one smooth motion. At the end of the day he would sit and smoke two cigarettes, allowing me a puff at the end of each. Then he would go back into the house and sit, lotus-legged, in front of the most newly decorated wall and nod, smiling gently, rocking back and forth.

"What is Japan like?" I asked him one evening as we were cycling home, my palms sweaty.

"Like everywhere else. Not as beautiful like this," he said, sweeping his arm around the fields and hills.

"Why did you come here?"

"So long ago." He pointed at his nose. "Don't remember. Sorry."

"Were you in the war?"

"You ask lots of questions."

"Somebody told me you were in Hiroshima."

He laughed uproariously, slapping his thighs. "These questions," he said. "I have no answer." He rode silently for a while. "Hiroshima was sad place. Japanese don't talk about."

"Were you in Hiroshima?" I asked again.

"No, no," he said. "No, no."

"Do you hate Americans?"

"Why?"

"Because . . . "

"You are very young. You shouldn't think these things. You should think of making good job with wallpaper. That's important."

We rode out to the house at eight every morning. The lawn was dry and cracked. The third-floor windows were black with soot. When the radio played it could be heard all over the house. Osobe worked with tremendous energy. In the hot afternoons I could see his sinewy arms under the sleeves of his rolled-up shirts. Once, when the radio told us of an earthquake in Japan, he blanched and said that the country was suffering from too much pain.

In the evenings I started going down to the bridge with my friends to drink flagons of cider with the money I held back from my parents. I began to buy my own cigarettes. I read books about World War II and created fabulous lies about how he had been in that southern Japanese city when the bomb had been dropped, how his family had been left as shadows on the Town Hall walls, all of them vaporized, disappeared. He had been ten miles from the epicenter of the blast, I said, in the shadow of a building, wearing billowy orange carpenter pants and a large straw hat. He was flung to the ground, and when he awoke the city was howling all around him. He had never found his family. They were scattered around the center, dark patches of people left on broken concrete. He had reeled away from the pain of it all, traveling the world, ending up eventually in the West of Ireland. My friends whistled through their teeth. Under the bridge they pushed the bottle towards me.

Occasionally my mother and father asked me about Osobe, muted questions, probings, which they slid in at dinnertime after I had handed over most of my wages.

"He's a strange one, that one," said my father.

"Hiding something, I'd guess," my mother would respond, the fork clanging against her teeth.

"Bit of a mad fellow, isn't he, Sean?"

"Ah, he's not too bad," I said.

"People say he lived in Brazil for a while."

"God knows, he could have," said my mother.

"He doesn't tell me anything," I said.

For all I really knew, he had just wandered to our town, for no good or sufficient reason, and decided to stay. I had an uncle in Ghana, an older brother in Nebraska, a distant cousin who worked as a well-digger near Melbourne, none of which struck me as peculiar. Osobe was probably just one of their breed, a wanderer, a misfit, although I didn't want him to be.

We worked through that hot summer together, finished the Gorman house, and started on a few others. I grew to enjoy clambering along the roads on our bicycles in the morning, slapping paste on the walls, inventing tales about him for my friends down under the bridge. Some of my friends were working in the chipper, others were bringing in the tired hay, and a couple of them were selling golf balls down at the club. Every evening I continued with Osobe stories for them, their faces lit up by a small fire we kept going. We all nodded and slurped at the bottles, fascinated by the horror and brilliance of it all. Fireballs had raged throughout the city as he fled, I told them. People ran with sacks of rice in their melted hands. A Shinto monk said prayers over the dead. Strange weeds grew in clumps where the plum trees once flowered and Osobe wandered away from the city, half-naked, his throat and eyes burning.

O sobe opened the door to me one morning toward the end of summer. "All the jobs almost done," he said. "We celebrate with cup of tea."

He guided me gently by the arm to the chair in the middle of the room. Looking around I noticed that he had been wallpapering again. He had papered over the paper. But there were no bubbles, no stray ends, no spilt paste around the edges. I imagined him staying up late at night, humming as he watched the patterns close in on him. The rest of the cottage was a riot of odds and ends—dishes and teacups, an oriental fan, wrapped slices of cheese, a futon rolled in the corner. There was a twenty-pound note sitting on the small gas heater near the table. Another ten-pound note lay on the floor, near the table. His brown hat was hung up over the door. There were paintbrushes everywhere.

"You did good job," he said. "Will you go soon school?"

"In a few weeks."

"Will you one day paper? Again. If I find you job?" he said.

Before I could answer he had sprung to his heels to open the
front door for a marmalade-colored cat, which had been scratching
at the door. It was a stray. We often saw it slinking around the back
of the chipper, waiting for some scraps. John Brogan once tried to
catch it with a giant net, but couldn't. It scurried away from everyone.
Osobe leaned down on his hunkers and, swooping his arms as if he
were going to maul it, he got the cat to come closer. It was almost a
windmill motion, smoothly through the air, his thin arms making
arcs. The cat stared. Then, with a violent quickness, Osobe scooped
it up, turned it on its back, pinned it down with one hand and
roughly stroked his other hand along it. The cat leaned its head
back and purred. Osobe laughed.

For a moment I felt a vicious hatred for him and his quiet ways,
his mundane stroll through the summer, his ordinariness, the ba-
nality of everything he had become for me. He should have been a
hero, or a seer. He should have told me some incredible story that
I could carry with me forever. After all, he had been the one who
had run along the beach parallel to a porpoise, who filled his pockets full of pebbles, who could lift the stray orange cat in his fingers.

I looked around the room for a moment while he hunched
down with the cat, his back to me. I was hoping to find something,
a diary, a picture, a drawing, a badge, anything that would tell me a
little more about him. Looking over my shoulder I reached across
to the gas heater, picked up the twenty-pound note and stuffed it in
my sock, then pulled my trousers down over it. I sat at the wooden
table, my hand shaking. After a while Osobe turned and came over
toward me with the cat in his hands, stroking it with the same harsh
motion as before. With his right hand he reached into his overalls and
gave me a hundred pounds in ten new notes. "For you school." I
could feel the other twenty-pound note riding up in my sock and as
I backed out the door a sick feeling rose in my stomach.

"You did very good job," he said. "Come back for visit."

It was only afterward that I realized I never got the cup of tea
he offered.

That night, I walked down along the row of houses where Osobe
lived. I climbed around the back of the house, through the hedge,
along by some flowerpots, rattling an old wheelbarrow as I moved
up to the window. He was there, slapping paste on the wall in
gentle arcs. I counted five separate sheets and the wall must have

come a good quarter of an inch closer to him. I wanted him to be sloppy this time, not to smooth the sheets out, to wield the knife in a slipshod way, but he did the job as always, precise and fluid. The whole time he was humming and I stood, drunk, rattling the change from the twenty-pound note in the bottom of my pocket.

Years later, when I was acquiring an English accent in the East End of London, I got a letter from my father. Business was still slow and a new wave of emigration had left its famous scars. Old Mrs. Hynes still hadn't kicked the bucket. Five of the new council houses were empty now and even the Gorman house had been sold once more. The American in his Cadillac had never arrived with his five blonde daughters. The hurling team had lost all its matches again this year. There was a bumper crop of hay.

On the last page of the letter he told me that Osobe had died. The body was not discovered for three days, until my old Aunt Moira called around with a basket of fruit for him. When my father went into the house he said the stench was so bad that he almost vomited. Children gathered at the front door with their hands held to their noses. But there was a whip-round made in Gaffney's pub that extended out to the streets. People threw generous amounts of money in a big brown hat that the owner of the chipper carried from door to door. My aunt chose him a fine coffin, although some- one said that he might have been offended by it, that he should have been sent back to Japan to be cremated. She scoffed at the sugges- tion and made a bouquet of flowers for him.

There was a party held the night of the funeral and rumors were flung around according to the depths of the whiskey bottle—but more or less everyone was sure now that he had been a victim of Hiroshima. All the young boys who had worked for him in the summer months had heard vivid details of that frightening August morning. He had fled from the city in a pair of wooden sandals. All his family had been killed. They had been vaporized. He was a man in flight. By the late, sober hours of the morning, my father added, the talk was that Osobe was a decent sort, no matter what his history was. Over the years he had employed many young men to work with him, treated them fairly, paid them handsomely, and confided in them about his life. They laughed at how strange his accent had become at the end of it all—when he went to the shop to buy cigarettes, he would lean over the counter and whisper for *pack of fags prease.* The sight of him carrying that big ladder on his bicycle would be sorely missed around town.

But the strangest thing of all, my father said, was that when he had gone into the house to recover the body, the room had seemed very small to him. It was customary to burn the bed sheets and scrape the paper from the walls when someone had been dead that long. But he took a knife to the paper and discovered it was a couple of feet thick though it didn't seem so at first glance. Layers and layers of wallpaper. It looked as if Osobe had been gathering the walls into himself, probably some sort of psychological effect brought on by the bomb. Because the wallpaper had been so dense my father and some members of the town council simply had to knock the house down, burying everything that Osobe owned in the rubble. There had been no clues in the house, no letters, no medical papers, nothing to indicate that he had come from that most horrific of our century's moments.

It was a pathetic gesture, but I rode my bicycle around London that night. I plowed along to no particular place, furious in the pedals. Blood thumped in me. Sweat leapt from my brow. The chain squeaked. A road in Ireland rose up—a road of grass grown ocher in the summer heat, a very thin figure in a brown hat along the river, a cat the color of the going sun, a certain wall brought forward in slow movements, a road that wound forever through dry fields toward a gray beach, a road long gone, a road flung out elsewhere, a road that was still within me somewhere. I found myself down by the Thames in the early morning—it was rolling along in a desultory gray. I dropped a single twenty-pound note into the water and watched it as it spun away very slowly, very deliberately, with the current, down toward some final sea, to fête the dead, their death, and their dying too.

AURA ROSENBERG

The Dialectical
Porn Rock

Aura Rosenberg's first intention was simply to play a joke on a fellow artist by leaving her rock sculptures, with their lacquered skins cut from porn magazine pages, by the stream where he regularly goes fishing. Her second intention was to reverse somehow the process of fetishism—to take inanimate objects and put the flesh back on them.

However, as part of Rosenberg's sculptural installations in the U.S. and Europe, these "porn rock découpages" were relocated from the physical landscape to various 'civilized' or cultural settings, where they became both jokes and fetish objects once again. By "planting" her rocks on the sites of manmade monuments and photographing them there, Rosenberg suggests that monuments, like jokes, can express more than one idea. By exhibiting the photographs, she invites the viewer to be the joker.

Rosenberg's working methods imitate and invert social methods of displacement. By focusing on the mechanics of transgression and suppression, she engages in the most transgressive act of all: she gives the joke away.

—Anne Doran

You See, I Love Life

1.

As the final recreational Thursday drew toward him like a gray station wagon cleaving the hot afternoon, he tore himself off his wailing dreams and began to arm, buying road maps on the sly, calling in a reservation on a travel bungalow across the state line. He was ready to give birth to his own brooding thoughts. Gliding over the slippery backs of days, he snatched handcuffs and tranquilizers, bought the right women's clothes, honed his smile-flashes sharp to do love's butchery again. Fortune's child like us all, he hummed with power like an electric drill only because Fortune had plugged him in. —No, the tense feeling of traveling alone into darkness is no worse than usual, he said to himself. It's just that I've gotten out of practice. —So they got in the sky-blue bus, counselors and inmates; they were going to the fair.

Win, win, win, win! the barkers shouted. Come on over! —The retarded ones cringed or laughed or shrieked for glee, gaping at the stuffed animals of every putrescent color which hung for prizes in love's abattoir; they were inside the fence now, tickets paid (a favor they'd never notice), hands stamped. —Group leaders! Group leaders! Pay *attention*, group leaders! We'll meet here at five-thirty sharp! Have a wonderful, wonderful time—

One of his charges was absent with a seizure—all the better for him. The other speechless ones could be disposed of with blinding pieces of change—here, for instance, where the phony canoes slammed down the river slide like a horrible torture. Strap them in: no malingering now ... Wipe the drool from their chins one last time, give them their meds a little early (a triple dose); slip the carnie man two twenties, presidential side up: Just keep them going round. I'll be back in an hour ... —As for the crowd, they were too busy pretending not to stare at the retards to notice *him*....

Fingers tight around her wrist. She turned to him full-face, ready to be led; he had the prize. Already the machine was starting up; over its roaring and clattering he could hear the speechless boys begin to bawl in fright. Well, they could bawl all they liked; not one would spill the beans—

Slipping his arm around her waist, he took her past the huddle of gray-clad security guards who lounged chuckling at the crackle of their own walkie-talkies, drinking Cokes, smoothing their greasy hair, glaring amiably at one another through ultra-dark sunglasses; no, they'd never remember him. He led her through the end of the afternoon swollen with light like some monster California orange, taking her where the heat and glare were fiercest, stalking through unknowing crowds, dodging her silently past girls throwing darts at balloons that resembled multicolored pustules (the girls hoped to win ugly pictures). She grunted softly and dug her feet in, twisting away from him to look back at the silver-studded ferris wheel whirring, gleaming fiercely in the sun. Then he saw that she was listening and sniffing for the scents of the other group leaders' cargo of differently ableds; some were up there whirling and gaping; just beside it, a number were strapped screaming to the giant pendulum on the pirate ride, raining down puke.... —Perhaps it was that that she sniffed and smelled. Did she remember their odors enough to miss them? —A barker was grasping air, wide-eyed, trying to grab him in. —Hey now let's go now let's play let's PLAY! Try it! —She turned her deadly gaze upon the barker, who said, "Hey, I'm sorry." —He took her away, the barker forlorn and sheepish, and he bought her a butterfinger-flavored slushy which she messed all down her dress and sticky hands, stretching her arms out to him like the bewildered parents stumbling down the children's rotating tunnel. He went and got electrocuted to win her a giant teddy bear which she went *awwwwrr* over and rubbed up and down against

147

her slushy-stained breasts while the yokels gawked, and then she retched, just a little yellow-brown tail of it sliding out of her mouth, and he wiped her on the bear and she started licking it back up and then she let the bear fall to the cement, poor Ursa Minor rolling, stinking and puke-matted in the hot sun with the flies already shooting down like bombers and her cheeks were blue and green where the bear's dye had come off. They were getting very far ahead of her lines now; they were going so far into his country that she'd never be coming back. The other inmates were long lost, the pirate ride out of sight; at the place where you throw baseballs at beer bottles he found a water fountain and cleaned her face a little; she slurped up the water and he let her drink until she was satisfied. Then he put her on a segment of a giant green caterpillar, riding beside her with his hand between her knees, and an old lady said to him: You're disgusting, taking advantage of that retard like that; and she said: *Worrrwww worrrww*. The ride ended full circle and he led her off, stalking deeper and deeper into the fair. Two women were hitting each other with giant inflatable crayons. A man in a white barbecue cap scratched his stubble crosswise and watched her. He drowned her in pools of sunlight, leading her into unknown valleys where the barkers shouted: There he is! —She was hugging her horse now on the merry-go-round, cawing and almost falling off, so he grabbed from his companion steed, saving her as they whirled past the SWIRL FRIES ten times a second; her mouth was open. She looked away, writhing her fingers....

2.

Hundreds of ribs and chickens burned on a giant glassed-in grill. Guys in baseball caps stood squirting them with hoses. She stumbled bowlegged behind him, finger-chained by him, her face gaping and grimacing, her tongue out. He bought her catfish on a stick. The lights were like horrid bathroom fixtures. She stopped dead to stare through the glass at the hulking girls in rainbow outfits, turning corn dogs in the roaring grease ... They saw her and started digging each other in the ribs and pointing, mouthing at her like fishes through the glass; he almost expected her lips to move silently back, but only a thick translucent thread of drool spun out.... Hands and tongues behind glass, the green-and-yellow depths of her lemonade cup, the bulging, pale pink nipples of the prize cow hanging straight down from the hairy, veined, and distended bag—all these and more, Virginia, swamped her marshy senses like stamping horses, pounding down the ooze inside her skull and galloping on while her darling forgetfulness oozed clear and fresh back up through the mud, washing it into its old featurelessness—or so he thought until they came to the pen of the giant sow. Giant, pink, and rosy-breasted, she offered many women's teats ranging along her in a double row, shaved and pink like a tender fat lady; and a big-eared piglet broke away from his litter mates nuzzled head to toe; he scuttled down the side of his mother, who twitched her cup-nose light years away from her own belly; he came to the rearmost teat and she ground him viciously down beneath her hind leg so that he squealed; but the rest of the farrow, more desperate than deterred, crowded suddenly down the whole long row of teats, grunting and swarming and stepping on each other, screeching like crows, passionately sucking, but at nothing, for she would not let her milk out; then and only then the retarded girl said *Urrrrwwwh!* and the great sow hunched her butt up, raised one abraded ear, turned her weary head, grunted: *Urrrrwwwh!* and let go, the dimples in her side rolling like waves, the young ones lining up straight and perpendicular now to nurse amidst that happy, tremendous, pink quaking—

3.

He escorted her on, past a stripe-aproned girl waving phosphorescent whips; people's backs went ahead, walking toward the orange-glowing tents. They were hours late now. The security guards would be looking for them. A Mexican, weary and sweating, turned barbecued turkey legs on a grill more shiny than the night, the meat glowing like fiesta condoms. He hurried her down the long bright sidewalk eyelashed with pole-lamp shadows, and there was a bench between the dance pavilion and the eggroll-on-a-stick booth where the moon teased her through the trees. He pulled her down on the dark grass white-wizened like an old dog's coat. Her face was a little blurred by the neon lights. Million-colored reflections of whirling blinked in the stagnant river beside them, lights going down escalators as his fingers strapped her cheeks bone-tight, pulling her easy lips open so that he could thrust his tongue, seizing her hair like reins, he rode her face the way he wanted to; the crossed thighs of the woman on the next bench reflected a winking light.... She beat her elbows frantically like a wounded bird. All around them, crowds sleepwalked through the lighted worlds as if they'd discovered the secret of happiness. The lights of the monorail rose between the trees where insects rattled. Wiping their mutual slobber from her face, he led her past another merry-go-round, now more lurid, the horses' mouths wide open in silent screams, the studded oval mirrors like blank mouths, the caterpillar statue turning dimly in the moonlight. The moon was over the porker pavilion, the smell of pig shit inside. The bleachers were crowded. He took her down in front to watch the races. A man with a hoarse beery voice was shouting: Go, red pig! Go, red pig! Fuck you in front, blonde bitch! Get down, get down! I said fuck you down in front, blonde bitch! Go, red pig! —and a man in a cowboy hat was easing his wheelchaired wife away from her reproachfully and the drunk came storming down because she was blocking his view. The drunk knocked her down with one fast punch that bloodied her nose and she started flailing silently on the floor, huge-eyed, cracking her head again and again on the concrete while he, the brilliant one, drew out his car keys, locked his fist around them with the longest one protruding between two fingers; then he stabbed the big drunk square in the eye once, twice, till something popped out. The drunk crashed down, curling tight around himself like a worm. Kicking him in the teeth, he leaped back, lifted her, ran with her until they'd hidden behind the couples with slurpies watching the goat being milked into the coffee can. Then they fled together, hand in hand, past luminous wheels and gears and lightbulb blooms and girls screaming in the night like witches being burned; with his dull-eyed bleeding prize he retreated across that battlefield of light. Yellow skeletons of light sucked children up and down as they screamed. Ferris wheels hummed like the reddish filaments of pulsating eyeballs—

4.

Inside she was as purple-pink and delicate as a puppy's tongue.

And she kept purring and cawing as he spread her thighs apart; she opened her mouth in surprise and grunted when he stuck it in: and she was so beautiful, even more so than the innocent girl, so beautiful that he could see that he was about to come almost right away; when he came it was as perfect as when he used to water the shrubs at the dream house, and from the hose came a rainbow, the gold band the widest, then the blue; when he turned the hose away, the rainbow endured for a half a second or so and then vanished; it seemed that the last drops falling out of empty air were gold or blue—

5.

The girl lay in the back seat sleeping with her hands over her ears, flushed, glistening with sweat, her bare arms almost white in the sunlight, her hair bleached to the color of very old bones. He whizzed her down the freeway between golden grass hills once virgin, now spiked with wire-boned power towers whose cables shattered the sky into meaningless polygons; he was taking her past where the gold and green hills turned yellow and blue. Surer now than all the spurting worms, he could unmask his memories of the long drive in lost years with his octopus-minded ex-wife; how he'd ridden silent and stunned in her hands' grip, knowing nothing other than that he was being borne away; now *he* was in charge, rushing an equally silenced prize home to his new lair, his treasure-house of all good things. The hacienda-roofed gas stations and motels rejoiced his heart; he knew they'd trip up any pursuers, wile away their eyes to slow them while he continued to speed his loved one to the place where even the sky's blueness bleached out. There was a spider on the back of his neck. She kept trying to make him pay attention to her. He wanted to pull over and suck her tongue right out of her mouth, but there wasn't time yet, not till he'd hidden beyond these almond orchards with the real estate developers' obscene signs already dooming them as they stood; once the trees had been cut down the police would be able to *see* farther, so he shot her through yellow tunnel light the color of lemon drops while she giggled and played with his hair and started gently smacking the top of his head making bird noises in rhythm with the slap; he pressed the gas pedal down a little more to explode them through the new buffer towns walled into compartments by rival developers, each tract with its own replicated roof; that was all that could be seen from outside, the wall rendering these neighborhoods into spurious Babylons of monotony— divine sites for a seraglio; even the inmates wouldn't know where they were; as for the authorities, they'd be baffled like the thieves in the *Arabian Nights,* eye-wandering that skyline of roofs along the endless road, locking wills with the palm trees that peeked over the wall.... She insinuated herself forward between the seats so that he couldn't see behind him and she tried to take his hand off the steering wheel to play with; when he wouldn't give it to her she started poking him and giggling. With alert spider-lashed eyes he peered into his rear-view mirror to make sure that no one was stalking him; then he twisted into a rest area, stopped, undid the seat belt, got into the back seat, and started kissing her as he'd wanted to do, dragging her down while she flapped her elbows in pleasure; he was wondering how to take her to the bathroom but just then she wet herself, so why bother. He put his hand up her sodden dress and she liked it; then he thought he heard a siren and leaped away from her, wiping the piss from his hands; he strapped her to the seat with a lap belt and handcuffed her wrists so she couldn't poke him anymore; then it was back to the golden hills crammed with sparkling cars, the yellow fever-hills of dying grass and barbed wire and planes, the hills eaten up by lethal new towns; rising out of his body as he hurtled down the four-lane highway past blondes and Komfort trailers, he achieved the Yum-Yum billboards and American flag bulldozing themselves bigger and bigger until they lost sight of their own emptiness, spouting out long low malls and bungalows to use up the flatness of needless space through which he drove like a pilot down a runway, between earth and air, dusted dry over his sweat; the car stank of her urine even when he rolled down the windows to let in the smells of the long flat green fields while she croaked in terror and distress, not understanding why she was restrained, why she couldn't have him; she was screaming and he had to roll the windows back up so that no one else would hear, and he heard the creaking of her struggling to get free, so he floored it to bring them faster and more safely past the blinding light of those yellow-green fields; at last he caught sight of the sought-for skyscrapers on their mutual horizon; he told her that they were almost there, but she didn't understand, crying and slobbering and biting her tongue and lips in a bloody frenzy of sadness as they roared past river-straddling cement bunkers, wolf packs of houses and bridges and cranes, a dead car on the shoulder, hood up like a penis, sawmills and two-story office cubes and more billboards and then long gray hot buildings to stupefy the skyscrapers, storage tanks, toxic factories half camouflaged by palm trees; and, slowing down block by block, he brought her into the "nice" neighborhood where there were fewer gas stations and more houses and trees—

6.

Once inside, he gave her two tranquilizers and rocked her to sleep. Then he locked her into the bedroom. He sprayed the back seat with stain remover and drove it to the carwash. Then he got some Kool-Aid and TV dinners. When he came back, he heard her sobbing and banging her head against the wall. He called her name and she sniffled into silence. Then he went into the kitchen to make her some Kool-Aid. He unlocked the bedroom door. As soon as she saw him come in, she started smiling and grunting and clutching at the folds of her pink dress—

7.

He took her into the backyard to play and the lady in the next bungalow came out and said: Who's that poor girl?

My sister's child.

As quickly as he decently could then, he pulled her back inside. He was one with a dog he'd once had that would always snap at cheese-wax thrown out of the window; getting what it craved into its jaws, the dog would immediately bound into the farthest corner of the yard for safe enjoyment, nothing there but dog and grass and cheese-wax, which left the dog in charge, by default . . .

8.

Studying the road atlas while she went *kaaaaw kaaaaw* at the TV, he wondered whether he'd be forced to unblur his ex-wife from memory on this drive, remembering the drive to their dream house when time and again she'd carved out her portion from his heart's crimson flesh. But his retarded girl, now, she was different; she couldn't strip him dead and bare; as for her, she came to him already stripped, like a live oyster on the half-shell; he didn't need to assault her; why he'd build her a castle, one of those ridiculous Disneyland castles with ice cream cone towers and a gaudy drawbridge of sighs . . . . He'd give her the whole teat: the illuminated foundations, eternal torches, the rush of blinking lights over sad-canted palm trees . . . Raising the blinds an inch, he saw that the sunset had come to the power poles. No neighbor lady in sight. Watered-down creamy clouds wobbled in "presenting" position, like drunken lambs dipped in orange dye. He played with her just as the shoe-shine boy rubs the gleaming loafers with a red cloth. When it was completely dark he drugged her nice and drowsy with a taste of gin and a half a sleeping pill. Then he hand-cuffed her wrists together and led her out to the car.

9.

The road was a weird windy segment of paleness as he drove her home to her perdition, only the double yellow lane in the center real, not the diamond-shaped hazard signs emblazoned with squiggly arrows to warn him of curves and pale trees. She picked at her seatbelt and cawed and tried to flap her elbows. —"That's right," he said, never looking away from the road. "That's right."—Gravel-cuts seized his gaze like something sticky, and the road was only darkness vanishing in a notch of monotony. The car bumped over moon-scarred asphalt the color of faded dreams, the darkness hot and unclean—

10.

They were very happy for weeks, until his money was gone. She needed to eat. He himself wasn't so hungry yet. Of course he would have gotten a job if he could, but leaving her alone made her shriek in grief and fear. So he had to work with her, as they said, not against her.

Well, there was one thing he could think of that she could do.

11.

The man peeled ten sticky five-dollar bills apart, fanned them, and laid them down on the counter. "I like to talk first," he said. "You mind if I talk first?"

"You better talk to me then. You won't get far talking to her."

The man leaned forward earnestly, wiped the sweat from his fore-head, and let air out of his mouth with a farting noise. "Well," he said, "I was raised never to be ashamed of who I am or what I do, and so I don't mind telling you that I'm a slapper. That's my job, and I'm proud of it. I'm hired to slap the babes around when they get out of line— only with an open hand, of course, never hard enough to really hurt 'em or knock 'em. A good slap is a slap you can see, though, a nice red handprint all up and down the cheek. They don't take it personally when I do it, because they know it's my job. A lot of 'em like me. I slap 'em on the ass, which coming from me is a compliment. Anyway, that's all I got to say. Where's the retard bitch?"

He watched the man go in, and the door closed. He heard the man lock the door on the inside. There was a long silence and then suddenly the sound of a slap. She was screeching hideously; suddenly the screams were muffled; the slapper must have stuffed her nightie or something into her mouth; then he heard the slaps as crisp and even as metronomic ticktock, heard her grunt trying to scream, heard the bed start creaking.

"One of my better ones," the slapper said, coming out. "A nice red handprint like a flower."

12.

The men went in and used her until their penises bowed like ducks' necks. They left little blotches of snow on her golden grass. A boy whose cheeks were burned purple in some industrial accident kept twisting around to look at the bedroom door when he went home. The entrepreneur said to himself: Everyone is defective, to live is to be imperfect. Didn't I once go kissing with a Mexican girl even though her legs were as hairy as tarantulas? —In these calculations he emulated the sixteenth-century Hochelagans, who were very greedy of wampum, which they used in their ceremonies. To get it they would kill a man and slit deep gashes in his body, which they then lowered into the river for ten or twelve hours. Upon hauling up the corpse, they could be confident that certain shellfish would have crawled inside these numb white cuts. From their exoskeletons the wampum was made. —He did not particularly enjoy the gashes which clients were now making in his sweetheart's soul, but at least she got to eat, lots of canned ravioli and gushy bland Spaghetti-O's . . . After a while he had money in the bank; then a taxidermist bought her outright, paid so well he couldn't refuse; oho, he was getting his own back now in love's unending war!

JANN MATLOCK

Delirious Disguises, Perverse Masquerades, and the Ghostly Female Fetishist

Woman can't be fetishists, declared psychiatrist Gatian de Gaeton de Clérambault, the future teacher of Jacques Lacan, in 1908. We might well welcome Clérambault's assessment. At last, after a century of analyses of female madness, doctors had found a form of abnormality from which women were exempt. Still, his conclusion seems odd, given that he might have found a good twenty female fetishists in the psychiatric literature of his time, and his insistence on gender difference in sexual madness reveals his ties to a century of observations of madness *in* difference.

Throughout the nineteenth century, *aliénistes* (as the members of the early French psychiatric movement called themselves) observed male and female patients through an optic that saw gender as the cause of illness. The midcentury psychiatric focus on hysteria—an illness only rarely found in men—doomed women to decades of surveillance, constraint, and inactivity, and prompted the much-asked question: Are women more prone than men to madness? During the 1880s, however, psychiatrists throughout Europe shifted their attention from hysteria to the various forms of perversion, and the old questions were replaced with new ones: Are women prone to perversion? Can women be fetishists too?

To understand how this psychiatric shift produced its own version of sexual difference, I have looked at two kinds of behavior identified as fetishistic perversion from 1880 to 1935: "clothing obsessions" and "costume obsessions." "Clothing fetishists" desire cloth or clothing, which they hoard, steal, masturbate with, and, in some cases, consider a prerequisite of sexual contact. "Costume obsessionals" desire sexual contact with partners wearing certain costumes, or want to dress themselves in certain costumes, frequently those of the opposite sex. These two kinds of "abnormality" focused concerns over homosexuality, masturbation, criminality, and degeneracy in turn-of-the-century France. They also played a central role in the development of perversion and a pivotal role in our understanding of sexual difference. Just as the mid-nineteenth-century debates about hysteria provided the foundation for the common understanding of women's sexuality, these later debates about clothing fetishism generated new perceptions of the body and the imagination.

Women hide their perversions better than men, argued *aliénistes* Jean-Martin Charcot and Valentin Magnan in the 1882 essay that first attempted to define sexual perversion. Clinical observations, however, demonstrated that "unnatural or contrary sexual impulses" were actually identical in both sexes—despite the fact that women might be better able to veil their "instinctive troubles."

As Magnan explained in 1885, there were four kinds of male and female *aliénés* demonstrating sexual aberrations: "idiots" suffering from the uncontrollable desire to masturbate; individuals unable to control their sexual urges for members of the opposite sex; "erotomaniacs" infatuated with some individual, imaginary or real, who occupied their every thought, though they remained chaste; and patients who experienced the same sentiments as "normal people" except that "for these individuals, the idea, the sentiment, or the penchant [was] *perverted.*" Unlike the masturbating idiots, convulsing nymphomaniacs, and vapid erotomaniacs, the last group of individuals proved particularly worrisome to Magnan and his contemporaries, because its members reasoned with agility and experienced their sexual urges in a simple, causal relationship to their chosen stimuli. Unlike the impoverished degenerates of the asylum, fetishists and perverts were frequently bourgeois or aristocratic, quite literate, and almost always in reproductive trouble.*

In the cases they saw:

A twenty-nine-year-old woman suffered from acute anxiety about her sexual desire for her five young nephews.

A thirty-two-year-old mother of two suffered from a sexual obsession with a thirteen-year-old schoolboy whom she had caressed, propositioned, and pursued, until the scandal convinced her family to place her in an asylum.

A young mother of three, despite her history of "morality and good conduct," announced to her husband that she had fallen in love with a youth of twenty-four, with whom she wished to spend six months satisfying her "needs of the soul" before returning to her conjugal duties.

An hysterical woman, harmoniously married for twelve years, fell wildly in love with a "cart driver," even though she was aware that her husband was "superior to her lover."

An engineer craved the sight of bottoms, especially those of little boys, and was so dismayed that he underwent shock treatments to his bone marrow in the hope that it would help him to fulfill his marital obligations.

A university professor suffered from an obsessional desire to see other men naked. His desires were accompanied by his pleasure in *la toilette féminine,* by cross-dressing, and talking about fashion with women.

Alfred Binet's 1887 essay "Le Fétichisme dans l'amour"—an attempt to explain the workings of "normal" love by understanding its pathological forms—studied lovers of the eyes, hands, hair, odors, voice, and, finally, "costume lovers": a handkerchief thief, a worshiper of nightcaps, a coveter of women's shoe nails, an adorer of white pinafores, a man who followed women wearing Italian dresses, and a hysteric who stole spoons, as well as men and women attracted to those of the same sex. Several of his cases involved women: a woman obsessed with a male singer's voice, a woman driven to sexual excitement by the ballet of Walpurgis, a woman obsessed with the desire

---

* The new emphasis on perversion also expanded the doctors' realm beyond the asylums where they practiced, and carried their sphere of influence into the privacy of bourgeois homes, where the clientele's financial means made psychiatric practice much more lucrative.

to cut out her child's tongue, and female characters from Barbey d'Aurevilly and Alexandre Dumas.

Two other cases, imported from Germany by Charcot and Magnan, proved the significance of at least one form of female fetishism: Both patients were young women who had shown a preference from an early age for other women. "They wanted to dress as boys, they would have wanted to be men. The gazes of certain girls impressed them acutely; they courted them, blushing when near them, struck by a keen passion." Cross-dressing, sexual desire for other women, masturbation, and suicidal wishes were enough to convince Charcot and Magnan of these women's psychopathic degeneracy.

As these cases and others like them reappeared in numerous other psychiatric studies over the next few decades, transvestism became the perversion psychiatrists were most willing to accord to women—even as they began to pay more attention to the varied forms of male cloth and costume fetishism. According to Binet, it was a woman's *clothing* and not her own sexual practices that had begun to characterize the obsessions attributed to male and female sexual perverts.

Men are driven to fetishistic madness by women, he explained: "One might say that every adornment and ornament that woman has invented, everything she has imagined as pretty, curious, bizarre, and extravagant to please a man, and vice versa, has been able to become the occasion of a new fetishism. Who can enumerate all the madness

caused by a beautiful red head of hair, or by the violent brilliance of a painted face?" Although women's artifice usefully encouraged the "normal" fetishism that enhances desire, Binet believed that when it became excessive, female ornamentation unhinged otherwise reasonable men.

Binet, however, left one question unanswered: how are doctors, lovers, or fetishists to know when women's displays have become too much? Where normal love is a "symphony" or "polytheistic fetish," he concludes, "the love of the pervert is a theater piece where a simple extra comes forward into the limelight and takes the place of the lead."

The greatest attraction of what we see, isn't it what we don't see? asked a turn-of-the-century opponent of women's dress reform. "Clothes make the body," declared Magnus Hirschfeld. The Berlin sexologist discovered that of one thousand (presumably "normal") men questioned by his institute, 65 percent preferred women either fully clothed (25 percent) or partially clothed (40 percent). He concluded with indignation that "the hypocrisy of our civilization" had "exerted a deplorable influence upon the sexual lives of men, for between this choice [of clothed women] and a pathogenic fetishism of clothes lies only a minimal difference."

When women tried to be men, the psychiatric profession of the late nineteenth century debated whether they were lesbians. When men tried to be women, psychiatrists puzzled over the sources of their attraction to clothes. Of a female transvestite, doctors asked: *Is she attracted to women? Is she hysterical? Does she have a history of degeneracy in her family? Has she ever shown any interest in the female social role?* Of a male transvestite, doctors asked: *Where did he first get his fascination with clothes like these? Does he actually want to wear the clothes or only to play with them, masturbate with them, and hoard them up in his drawers? Does he steal women's clothes? What does he do when he wears the clothes? Does he imagine he is female or does he pretend he is a man desiring the woman he sees in the mirror? What does he fantasize about?* Throughout fifty years of analyzing transvestism, doctors echoed a repeated desire to know more about the toilette of the men in question. Their analyses of female cross-dressers took the women's choice of clothing as a given, and went straight to their other sexual and social propensities.

Is this because men's clothes simply weren't very interesting? Since what J. C. Flugel, in his influential but questionable study *The Psychology of Clothes* (1930), called the eighteenth century's "Great Renunciation," when men shed their peacock apparel and chose staid, dark, proper clothing to mark their social seriousness and breeding, men's clothing has permitted few fantasmic touches in style, color, or fabric. Draping the body, but rarely emphasizing its shapes, and geared to the utilitarian, men's clothes have simply never been much fun. When women put them on, they become a disguise that masks all that was seen in the nineteenth century as feminine, attractive, and coquettish. Did doctors pay so much attention to their male cross-dressers' toilette because they found the nuances of women's clothing more compelling? Or because, like their patients, they found an irresistible attraction in women's garments?

"We are all more or less fetishists," admitted *aliéniste* Émile Laurent in 1896. "Every woman whom a man loves in his heart is forcibly a little bit of a fetish."

Woman, because of her physical makeup, is made to be draped, not to be molded, argued Émile Blavet, a late-nineteenth-century opponent of men's wear for women. "Anything that deviates from the drape and approaches the tight-fitting is antiartistic. In a man's suit, a woman is no longer a woman, and she is not a man: she is an androgyne, which is to say she's something undefined, unsexual, less troubling than odious."

Beginning in 1800, police permission was legally required for all women who wished to wear pants on the Paris streets at any time other than carnival, but such restrictions seem only rarely to have been enforced before the 1880s, and only a handful of women— among them Napoleon III's mistress, Marguerite Bellanger, and the painter Rosa Bonheur—actually requested a permit. What had been acceptable, even titillating, in the July Monarchy, however, came to be seen, during the Third Republic, as pathological, immoral, and threatening to the social order. By the late nineteenth century, regular reports of scandals and arrests of women who had flouted the law began to appear in the press. In 1882, a press report recorded that some women caught cross-dressing without permission had been tried and sentenced to imprisonment. According to police records of the time, only ten women possessed police permits—not particularly surprising considering that the police required a doctor's testimony that male clothes were necessary to the woman's health.

Three kinds of female masqueraders appear in the psychiatric and police annals of the time. Two of them, asylum inmates and gender "frauds," proved worrisome well before the end of the century, as analysts believed these women endangered themselves and those around them with their sexual confusion. The third kind of masquerader garnered her dangers from the psychiatric turn to perversion. And she, more than all the other perverts catalogued, attracted attention to her *social* as well as *sexual* role.

Until the 1880s, a woman's request to wear men's clothes had not in itself constituted a rationale for her family or the police to bring her to the Salpêtrière, the public psychiatric asylum for women in Paris. In order to become a psychiatric case, a cross-dressing woman had had to do far more than spend her days primping, whereas a man's cross-dressing alone seems to have been enough to enlist the help of an *aliéniste.*

In April 1845, a woman was brought to the Salpêtrière in a delirium: "She doesn't know her own sex," the admitting doctor wrote. Another woman, in 1852, had manic delusions of being Napoleon. The famous *aliéniste,* Étienne Esquirol, described a woman whose frenzies were calmed by a change of dress:

> Madame M....was very agitated, talking nonstop, insisting and repeating heatedly that she was not a woman but a man. If someone speaking to her called her "Madame," she immediately became more agitated, swearing or indulging in violent behavior. [A superintendent] arranged with Doctor Pinel to get men's clothing for this woman: she put on these clothes with raptures of joy, and strolled ostentatiously among all her companions; she was calmer, more tranquil, and talked much less, but she got furiously excited if someone did not call her "Monsieur"...

In their attempts to diagnose these three cases of female transvestism, the only such cases I have encountered in French psychiatric studies before the 1880s, the *aliénistes* simply gave voice to the content of their patients' desires.

By the fin de siècle, however, the conditions for becoming a psychiatric subject had drastically changed: cross-dressed women began to enter psychiatric texts simply through their arrest by the police. And sexologists such as Krafft-Ebing, Hirschfeld, and Moll report as "observations" cases culled from newspapers, police reports, foreign medical journals, and other doctors' studies—frequently also the results of police intervention. Whereas at mid-century Dr. Ulysse Trélat could claim to have witnessed nearly every one of the seventy-seven patients he included in his *Folie lucide*, doctors of the turn of the century exchanged patients' case studies like baseball cards.

A popular actress was discovered to be male after "her" death. The reigning queen of a society ball was also unveiled as male. The proliferating cases of women who had lived as men left doctors even more indignant. For the women to elude discovery implied a breakdown in the order on which doctors and police depended. Doctors emphasized the inevitable failure of disguises: "an 'invert' dressed as a boy and pretending to be a young man, succeeded, through ardent fervors, in winning the love of a normal young girl, and became engaged to her. But shortly after, this woman crook was unmasked, arrested, and taken to an insane asylum for observation. There," Dr. Auguste Forel reported, "I had him dressed again in women's clothes." Krafft-Ebing analyzed the case of another nearly successful impostor who swindled the father of her bride out of a sum of money. When 'Count Sandor' was discovered to be "no man at all, but a woman in male attire," she was arrested and brought to trial. Acquitted as not responsible for her acts and sent home, she "again gave herself out as Count Sandor." Krafft-Ebing also treated for her "viraginity" a charwoman who had engaged herself to a young girl "under the pretext that she was a man and belonged to an aristocratic family." Under Krafft-Ebing's care, "she bewailed the fact that she was not born a man, as she hated feminine things and dress generally." He also reported a case of a Wisconsin woman who had "eloped in 1883 with a young girl, married her, and lived with her as husband undisturbed"—presumably until it was discovered that the body she had remade did not correspond to social standards.

Some women acknowledged that they wore their masquerades to achieve parity with men. In 1889, the Parisian press reported a case of a woman brought before the Paris police commissioner for having passed herself off as a man for the preceding ten years: "She told . . . the judge that she had left Strasburg, where she left her husband because of 'incompatibility of temper,' and arrived in Paris [in 1878]. The man who carried her off had a printshop; soon she entered into partnership with her lover, and from then on she wore a man's suit, which, she said, allows women to devote themselves more freely to the tasks of business." What surprised everyone, from the police to the press, was that this woman had pursued her business affairs for ten years "without anyone ever noticing her counterfeit presence." When the judge explained to her that she was breaking the law, she apologized, explaining that she was unaware of the law, and expressed the desire to request the prefecture's permission henceforth to wear men's clothes.

"Fashion constructs female subjectivity and female sexuality," cultural critic Kaja Silverman reminds us. In rejecting nineteenth-century fashion dictates, these women chose to construct their own subjectivity and sexuality within an order they found acceptable for their goals and desires. Most striking in the discussions of these women's choices, however, is that we never learn *how* they reappropriated the fashion of their new roles. Can their masquerades have been that boring? Did the doctors simply choose to look away?

Transvestite men are the most horrible of women, Dr. Louis Reuss asserted in 1886: "The male invert gathers in himself the worst faults of women." When Jacques-François Renaudin was arrested for wearing women's clothing, in 1846, however, police found no laws prohibiting his attire. To avoid "public polemics," the police chief requested that his officers leave Renaudin alone "unless beneath the clothes of a woman he should commit a public outrage to modesty."

Despite the absence of laws against such behavior, cases of cross-dressing men far outnumber those of women in French as well as German psychiatric studies of the fin de siècle. We know from police prefecture psychiatrist Paul-Émile Garnier's observations that by the last decade of the century, men were regularly arrested for clothing obsessions: "One day they brought to the special infirmary a young butcher, Louis J., whose accoutrements were among the most singular. Under a full coat he was wearing: a blouse made of black cloth, a corset bottom, a corset, a camisole, a collerette, a knit of light fabric, and finally a woman's blouse. He also wore fine stockings and garters." Louis had been collecting women's underwear for years—and had reduced himself to poverty through his expensive acquisitions. At the police infirmary, he begged Garnier unsuccessfully to "authorize" him to wear women's clothing.

Garnier's study reminds us of the power of fashion to entice men as well as women into its web. An unidentified man of letters followed prostitutes, seduced by the richness of the costume he was convinced lay beneath their outer garments. What enchanted him was "all that is fine, elegant, coquettish; it is the *envelope* of the woman that pleases him and not the woman herself...." "I would have wished," the man explained, "for the sake of modesty, to be ladies' maid to an elegant woman of the world, to help my mistress undergo four dress changes each day, or to undergo four for myself."

Garnier appealed for help for these men, whom he believed doomed by their "degeneracy" to commit acts viewed as criminal by social norms. Like the kleptomaniac who stole nightcaps because he desired their odor, the fetishist who broke into homes to steal the women's underwear which he applied to his genitals, and the silk fetishist who couldn't stop himself from stroking women who were wearing the fabric he desired, Garnier's cross-dressers were fetishistic obsessionals, irresistibly drawn to cloth and clothing out of a desire for a "contact which sums up for them sensual beatitude." The "envelopes" of women, which so pleased them, belonged to the domain of artifice and coquetry. They had been enticed into the theater of illusion.

Qui culotte a, liberté a, runs an old proverb, "Who has the pants has freedom." Novelist George Sand, actress Sarah Bernhardt, and traveler Isabelle Eberhardt appropriated the guise of men not to play with sexuality but simply to enjoy the ease of movement it afforded. In the 1880s, however, the freedoms associated with wearing pants suddenly became a terrifying specter for the French middle classes. What had changed? First, increasing pressure for improvements in women's legal and social status reminded conservatives what might be at stake if women were granted unconditional bodily self-determination. Second, the Franco-Prussian War and the Commune had left the French terrified lest the next war bring an end to the "French race," and the ever-decreasing birth rate upped the ante on women's feminine and maternal essence. Doctors made certain to note that women clothing obsessionals had abandoned husbands and even children, demonstrating a lack of commitment to reproduction.

Clothes might remake desires, doctors and moralists worried. The "theater of gender" into which psychiatry needed to cast women depended increasingly upon their participation in masquerades designed for heterosexual excitement. As historian Thomas Laqueur has shown, this meant "man-made" sexual distinctions that allowed no tinkering: "The power of culture thus represents itself in bodies, and forges them, as on an anvil." In nine-teenth-century France, the power of culture represented itself as well in the shrouds that enveloped bodies, forging them in ways that might control the bodies within.

"To avoid being noticed when dressed as a man, one must already be accustomed to avoiding notice when dressed as a woman," wrote George Sand. Although women's excessive vanity had been criticized throughout the nineteenth century, by the turn of the century, doctors and moralists seemed to have given up the fight. So what if bourgeois women had learned their fashion tricks from prostitutes? Who cared if working-class women put on airs? As long as women kept their hands where they "belonged," engaged in their conjugal duties, and behaved themselves in public, they might appropriate any female fashion they saw fit. But just as women began to gain control over female fashion, psychiatrists sounded new alarms: Women had started to shoplift, and the number of klepto-maniacs was increasing dramatically.

Ll women are clothes fetishists, Freud concluded: "Even the most intelligent women behave defenselessly against the demands of fashion." Other psychiatrists argued that kleptomaniacs were the female equivalents of male fetishists. Succumbing to the desire for masquerade, spectacle, and theater which surrounded them, these women were seduced into collecting the objects that even they knew could not mask what they lacked.

Many doctors insisted that kleptomania was related to menstrual syndromes and menopause. Some attributed the rash of department store thefts to hysterics' capriciousness, their criminal nature, and their coquettish instincts. Others theorized that department stores "contain and spread out before desirous gazes the richest of materials, the most luxurious items of dress and the most seductive inessentials." What woman could resist these temptations, *aliéniste* Henri Legrand du Saulle asked: "Women of all circumstances—attracted into these elegant surroundings by the natural instincts of their sex, fascinated by so many foolhardy provocations, dazzled by the abundance of lace and trinkets—find themselves overtaken by a

sudden incitement, not premeditated, but almost savage: they put a clumsy yet furtive hand on one of those displayed items, and there they are, improvising as thieves." Yet the doctors who recorded these proliferating cases of female kleptomania seemed to forget that one can never have *enough* of illusion. Just as there were endless ways to mask faults or to ornament forms in search of the illusions that would tempt men to reproduction, one could find in any department store enough fabric, fur, lace, jewels, ribbons, and makeup to drive desiring women to distraction. Doctors had long applauded the successful artifices women use to ornament their beauty. Now they imprisoned women for pilfering those very items they had been urged to desire.

The fetish has traditionally been seen as an object that allows its desirer to maintain a fantasy of *presence*, even when all signs point to absence. The fetish magically creates the illusion that nothing is amiss even when no rational power remains for belief. Female fetishists threaten for the same reasons female cross-dressers scandalize: because they subvert the lines between gender that are supposed to tell an irrefutable story of primal difference. Most of all, female fetishists threaten, as Clérambault's study shows, because they invest clothes, objects, and even knowledge with desires that can be pirated only with their consent.

If a man rubs a fetish object against his genitals, Clérambault calls the act coitus. If a woman does so, Clérambault labels her act masturbation. The man's act puts in motion "all the physical and moral factors of male love while the woman's . . . is far from putting into play all the elements of sensuality." Male fetishists have a remarkable arsenal of tricks, Clérambault believes. They can summon "splendid" imaginary scenes during masturbation and coitus, "transforming reality in their thoughts, enriching it and ennobling it." The three female cloth obsessionals whom Clérambault analyzed in 1890, however, seem to achieve none of the splendor, richness, and nobility of their male counterparts: "They masturbate with the silk without any more reverie than a solitary epicure savoring a fine wine; in the absence of any pieces of silk, they do not dream of sumptuous silks; to help them masturbate they do not supplement the touch of the silk with visions of people dressed in silk, nor do they imagine themselves jumping wantonly into an abundance of various silks." For these three women, silk has a "purely" tactile appeal. For men, Clérambault believes, the fetish object is "all of a person." For women, it is just a thing for rubbing.

To read Clérambault's contemptuous portrait of female cloth obsessionals, one might think that male fetishism was a feat to attain. Women's relationships to their pseudofetish objects are barren ones indeed: "In their contact with the silk, they are passive; their personality is closed to the outer world, stripped of vision, stripped of desire; the opposite sex does not exist anymore; their orgasm is indeed genital, but it satisfies so much for itself that one could call it asexual." Clérambault's women—all diagnosed as hysterical and all driven to masturbate with the cloth they steal—are not fetishists, but rather cases that he places "next to fetishism and in its shadow." What Clérambault rejected as inferior about his female "fetishists" was the *quality* of their fantasies (although he describes all of these women as having an unusual propensity for "the most fantastical reveries").

What convinces the doctor of the inferiority of women's fetishistic practices? Quite simply the fact that these women's fantasies have nothing to do with the particular piece of silk. The silk hasn't been anywhere the women care about or belonged to anyone they desire. It has no past, no future. It evokes no associations. It tells no stories. It leaves the doctor without a clue to the imaginations of his patients. It withholds from him all the fantasies he could plunder and the desires he could believe he understood.

Nineteenth-century gender relations took place in a theatrical realm in which all desire was mediated by the trappings of consumer culture. In such a "theater of gender," as this essay has shown, the clothes that "made" a woman's body could generate female as well as male fantasies. Her deviations from those fantasies, her rejection of the masquerades of femininity, however, marked her as perverse. She had not dressed for her part.

The nineteenth century defined two kinds of cross-dressing for men and women, and divided them across gender lines. Masquerade—putting on an extra layer of display—ultimately became the realm of women in this theater of gender, while disguise—the art of the cover-up—came to define the pathologized form of female transvestism. Male masquerades—men who wanted to be female—were seen as monstrous since doctors believed that no one in his right mind would have such aspirations. Male disguises, by contrast, emerged as the cornerstone of both nineteenth-century fashion and moral behavior. The man was not allowed to put on a show, but he could put one over on anyone he liked, and was applauded for bringing the masquerades of others into his service. Double identity, double entendres, even double lives, were acceptable for any man who could master their challenges. Woe to the nineteenth-century woman who tried to live a double life. She would be better served by ripping off fine dresses from department stores: at least she could always say she didn't need the second skin they might have afforded her. As for the nineteenth-century woman caught trying to live duplicitously, even her masquerades would not save her from the police, doctors, and popular opinion.

That doctors like Clérambault and his twentieth-century followers were so hesitant to accord women a place in the annals of fetishism should not, however, make us wish to reclaim one. The stories told of male and female fetishists and transvestites at the time were desperately imprisoning ones, one-way tickets to asylums, prisons, and other social constraints. Rather, one might want to use the history of psychiatric obsessions at the fin de siècle as a reminder of the powers we lodge in bodies and the secrets we can keep hidden in the shrouds forged around them. That, in our own society, masquerades, disguises, and fetishes still maintain such a fascination should assure us that we are not done with the matter of bodies, or with the need to share secrets, ever so cautiously, through our own manipulation of the illusions we call gender.

Author's note: This article is an adapted version of a longer piece which appeared as "Masquerading Women, Pathologized Men: Cross-Dressing, Fetishism, and the Theory of Perversion, 1882–1935," in Fetishism as Cultural Practice, *edited by Emily Apter and William Pietz (Cornell University Press). Complete citations for all quoted material may be found there. All citations from the French are my own. Thanks for their help with the original version go especially to Emily Apter, William Pietz, Jacques Postel, and the staffs of the Bibliothèque Henri Ey, the Paris Archives de la Préfecture de Police, and the Archives de l'Assistance Publique. Clues to what cloth fetishes evoked for Clérambault himself can be found in Joan Copjec's "The Sartorial Superego,"* October, 50 (Fall 1989).

Another Life

Women spend the afternoon squatting on the porch
     picking lice from each others' hair,
they spend the evening feeding the little ones
     and lulling them to sleep in the glow of the bottle lamp.
The rest of the night they offer their backs
     to be slapped and kicked by the men of the house
or sprawl half-naked on the hard wooden cot—

Crows and women greet the dawn together.
Women blow into the oven to start the fire,
tap on the back of the winnowing tray with five fingers
     and with two fingers pick out stones.

Women spend half their lives picking stones from the rice.

Stones pile up in their hearts,
there's no one to touch them with two fingers . . .

Translated from the Bengali by
Carolyne Wright with Farida Sarkar

Body Theory*

This body of mine, known so long,
at times even I can't recognize it.
If a rough hand
with various tricks touches my hand smeared with sandalwood paste,
in the house of my nerves a bell chimes,
      a bell chimes.

This my own body,
this body's language I can't read;
it tells its story itself in its own language.
Then fingers, eyes, these lips, these smooth feet,
none of them are mine.
This hand is mine only
yet I don't correctly recognize this hand;
these lips are mine only, these my breasts, buttocks, thighs,
none of these muscles, none of these pores
are under my command, under my control.

In the two-story house of my nerves
      a bell chimes.
Then in this world whose plaything am I,
man's or Nature's?

---

* The Bengali for "body theory" is *dehatattwa*, a Sanskrit-derived term which can also
mean "anatomy" or "physiology." The more immediate associations of *dehatattwa*
for a Bengali reader would be the Tantric doctrine that the body is the seat of all
knowledge, and its esoteric implication that sexual acts can thus be employed as
spiritual exercises in the search for union with the Divine.

In fact not man
but Nature plays me,
I am the *sitar* of its whims.

At man's touch, I
wake up, breaking out of my slumbering childhood;
in my sea, a sudden high tide begins.
If the sweet scent of love is found in my blood and flesh,
it's Nature only that plays me,
I am the *sitar* of its whims.

Translated from the Bengali by
Carolyne Wright with Mohammad Nurul Huda

Family Secrets

Morton Bartlett was born in Chicago, Illinois in 1909. He attended Phillips Exeter Academy and Harvard University, then settled in Boston, where he worked as a free-lance advertising photographer, gas station manager, traveling furniture salesman, decorative painting instructor, and finally as a print and design coordinator. During the thirty-year period from 1935 until the mid-1960s, Bartlett sculpted a family of fifteen children (twelve girls and three boys, aged eight to sixteen), ranging from half lifesize to scale. He made clothes, provided the sculptures with wigs of real hair, posed them, and took over a hundred photographs of them. When he died in 1992, at the age of 83, his sculptures were found separately packed in handmade boxes. The only time Bartlett discussed his work in public, in an interview he gave to *Yankee Magazine* in 1962, he explained that each figure took almost a year to create, each head several months more, and that the sculptures were based on *Gray's Anatomy* as well as photographs of real children from the 1930s. According to friends and neighbors, these figures served as a kind of surrogate family for Bartlett, who was orphaned at the age of eight. Listing sculpture as his hobby in the Harvard Class of 1932 *25th Anniversary Report*, he explained, "Its purpose is that of all proper hobbies—to let out urges which do not find expression in other channels." Bartlett's will named various children's charities as the beneficiaries of his estate.

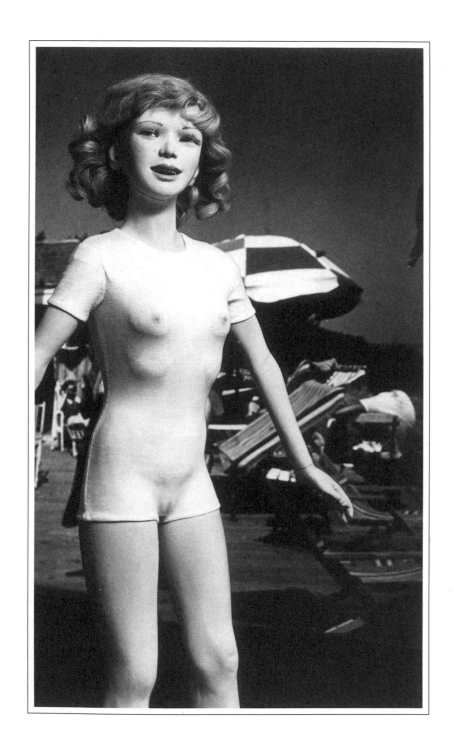

Footsucker

I love feet. They talk to me. As I take them in my hands I feel their strengths, their weaknesses, their vitality, or their failings. A good foot, its muscles firm, its arch strong, is a delight to touch, a masterpiece of divine workmanship. A bad foot—crooked toes, ugly joints, loose ligaments moving under the skin—is an agony. As I take these feet in my hands I am consumed with anger and compassion: anger that I cannot shoe all the feet in the world, compassion for all those who walk in agony.

Salvatore Ferragamo, Shoemaker of Dreams

Just as the fetish enables the fetishist to simultaneously recognize and deny woman's castration, irony allows the ironist to both reject and reappropriate the discourse of reference.

Naomi Schor, "Fetishism and its Ironies," in Nineteenth-Century French Studies, *Fall 1988*

Put on your red shoes and dance the blues.

David Bowie, "Let's Dance"

I held her feet in my hands. They were perfect, of course; as pale and pure and cold as vellum. I kissed them, let my lips move softly and dryly over their insteps, then placed them gently on the floor by the bed. I took a final long, lingering look. I wanted always to remember them this way.

Then I took a claw hammer, previously unused, all shiny burnished steel, and a rubber sheath around the handle, to give grip and absorb shock. I raised it high above my head, let it balance at the peak of its apex, and then I brought it down as hard and as precisely as I could, down onto the cold, pale, white left foot. I did it again for the right. Then several times more, again and again until the feet were no longer perfect, indeed no longer recognizable as feet, until they were smashed, disordered, pulverized, scattered to all points of the room.

White dust hung low in the air. White fragments littered the floor, and I gathered them together, crumbling them between my fingers. Of course there was no blood, no flesh, no splinters of bone, no smashed tissue. All I had done was destroy two plaster casts of Catherine's feet. The real ones were still intact, still perfect, although they were no longer accessible to me.

I had hoped that destroying the casts might act as a kind of therapy, as a kind of voodoo. I had hoped that destroying the replicas might also destroy the hold that Catherine's feet had over me. As I sat on the floor surrounded by plaster rubble, I knew that the magic hadn't worked. I was as deeply in thrall as ever.

An anatomist would tell you that the foot is a terminal part of the inferior extremity, what you and I would call the leg. He would say the foot serves as a support structure and also as an instrument of locomotion. He would say that the foot is divided into three sections, the tarsus, the metatarsus, and the phalanges; that there are seven tarsal bones, five metatarsal bones, fourteen phalangeal bones, a total of twenty-six.

He would say that the foot is intricately and richly supplied with muscles, blood vessels, and nerves. Only some of these are responsible for making the foot an object of fascination to a man such as myself. For instance, on the dorsal surface of the foot you will find the extensor brevis digitorum, a thin broad muscle that subdivides to form four tendons that spread out across the foot. On any foot that I found truly beautiful these tendons would have to be clearly, tautly visible.

Also on that same surface you find the dorsalis pedis artery, a vessel which splits and forms branches, the tarsi and metatarsi which run parallel across the top of the foot, and the introsseae and dorsalis hallucis which run along the foot in the direction of the toes. These too stand out in low relief on a beautiful foot.

Then there are the internal and external plantar nerves which crisscross the foot again branching and subdividing, interweaving with bone and muscle. These are not obviously visible but it is these that are responsible for making the foot so uniquely sensitive.

But an anatomist, for all his knowledge of the structure and internal workings, would not be used to making aesthetic judgments about the foot, whereas I used to spend my whole time doing precisely that.

Let me see if I can describe the perfect pair of women's feet. Certainly they would need to be long and lean. A thick layer of fat around the foot hides its character. They should not be too small and neat in case they look too childlike and innocent—that is anything but sexy. They should look strong and active. They should have high arches and lean, narrow ankles.

Obviously, these perfect feet will be healthy, free from growths, scars, deformities, without hard or discolored or flaky skin. However, I am not averse to a foot having a lived-in look. A lifetime of wearing high heels and exotic shoes will inevitably leave a few traces, and these are not to be despised.

The flesh may be stark white or beautifully tanned, but as I say, in either case, the bones, tendons, and veins must be visible through the skin, rippling and articulating as the foot moves. Occasionally one sees a foot that looks as taut and veined as an engorged penis. Or is it the other way round? That is the kind of foot I lust over. That is the kind of foot Catherine had.

The toes need to be long, straight, and slender. They should never be plump or bulbous. Twisted or overlapping toes are hideous, and despite the examples we see in Renaissance and Greek sculpture, I like the first toe to be shorter than the big toe.

The nails are all-important. The perfectly shaped foot can be ruined by bad nails, and the prime factor here is shape. They must not be spatulate. They should be the shape of tiny television screens rather than of seashells. They should be large in relation to the size of the toe, centrally and symmetrically placed. They should be without ridges and free from cuticle debris. They should be kept long rather than cut short and, of course, they should be painted. The range of acceptable colors runs a comparatively narrow spectrum, from dark pink to deep maroon, and my personal preference is for something approaching Porsche red. White, silver, metallic, and pearl finishes are totally dreadful. I always think that black polish should deliver a certain frisson, yet

I find it never quite does. Greens and purples seem merely odd and unnatural, and if it seems strange to talk about nature in this cosmetic context, I think that what we're actually dealing with here is nature red in claw if not in tooth.

Foot jewelry has always struck me as a gilding of the lily. Likewise painting the feet with henna seems an unnecessary, and not especially sexual, complication. I can see that a small tattoo on the foot could have a certain erotic charge, but I have always felt that the perfect foot would not be tattooed, and Catherine's certainly was not.

I realize, of course, that laying down laws for female beauty is an absurd and dangerous occupation. And if I sound dogmatic and impossibly demanding, all I can say is, sorry, but that's how it is with fetishes. Of course, feet that do not conform to my ideal have every right to exist and to be admired. Indeed I myself have admired and been intimate with feet that were a long way from perfect. Nevertheless, a man knows what he wants. And in one sense I am being descriptive rather than prescriptive, for as I describe my idea of the perfect foot, I find that I am, of course, very precisely describing Catherine's.

But the perfect foot is not bare. It is shod. The shoe delivers a vital aesthetic transformation. It customizes a part of the body. Whereas the perfect foot allows only one possibility, there are an infinite number of shoes that may be admired and enjoyed. Shoes can be bought, they can be specially made, but the perfect foot is a natural phenomenon like the Grand Canyon or Victoria Falls.

Of course the shoes need to be high-heeled, the higher the better, within reason. I don't personally feel any need to psychoanalyze the high heel but undoubtedly it makes women stand and walk differently. It raises their buttocks and it makes them wiggle. It makes them look high and mighty, but at the same time it makes them quite vulnerable. It is hard for them to run away. Hence the term "fuck-me shoes," or FMs as I prefer to call them; i.e., the woman is saying if you can catch me you can fuck me, and, of course, any damn fool can catch a woman in a pair of shoes with six-inch heels.

This does not sound politically correct, I know, indeed it can sound downright misogynistic, but hey, I didn't invent the term or the concept. As a matter of fact, the first time I ever saw the phrase "fuck-me shoes" in print was in Shelley Winters' autobiography, *Shelley, Sometimes Known as Shirley.*

She tells how, in her early career, she and Marilyn Monroe used to steal shoes from the studio to wear dancing. They were high-heeled sandals with a kind of lattice work at the toe and an ankle strap tied in a bow, and she refers to them as fuck-me shoes. She says, "They really were the sexiest shoes I've ever seen. Whenever we did pinup photos for the soldiers, we wore them."

Like Shelley, I'm a great fan of the ankle strap, and even more so of the double ankle strap. I'm absolutely sure this must have something to do with bondage and restraint, and it is echoed in thongs, and even in certain kinds of laces. All of these are very welcome.

Fabrics may vary, but only within certain limits. I tend to like my women's shoes to be made of something that was once alive: leather or suede, snake or alligator skin, tiger, antelope, or, as in Catherine's case, zebra. But I am not too dogmatic about this. I also enjoy velvet, silk, and satin. Synthetic fabrics are not a source of pleasure for me. Perspex, plastic, Bakelite, are not on my erotic map, and neither are raffia, wood, or rubber.

Color is again important. My taste is toward strong colors, reds and blacks above all, but purples and blues are fine too. Earth tones, beiges, yellows, and grays really don't do it, and white shoes are, of course, simply absurd.

I am something of a classicist in my choice of shoes. I like them to be bold and uncluttered. I go for the sweep rather than the telling detail. I like them to be hard-edged, smooth, streamlined. I really don't have much time for fussiness, for buckles and bows, buttons, beadwork, rhinestones, sequins, artificial flowers. On the other hand I am very prepared to be entertained by a mule, a slingback, a strappy sandal, a fur slipper. Much as I like the straight stiletto, I am still an admirer of the comma heel and the *talon choc.*

There is, however, a whole category of shoe that is simply unerotic. Included here are the clog, the trainer, the flip-flop, the Dr. Scholl exercise sandal. We need not concern ourselves with these except to note that my dislike of them indicates the extent to which my fetishism is concerned with aesthetics, not with function or proximity. It's not the *idea* of the foot or shoe that's important to me, it's the reality, the sight, the touch, the form.

I have nothing against boots, whether they run to the ankle, to the calf, the knee, or the thigh, and I'm well aware that a whole category of fetishists worships them. But they fail to work for me simply because they enclose and therefore hide the foot. They conceal the object of desire. This might be a good thing if your sexual partner had ugly feet, I suppose, but how could you live with such a partner? How could you have sex with her?

What a good shoe crucially does, must do, is reveal the foot, enhance and display it, offer a frame and a setting for it. And this is precisely the nature of my erotic obsession. I crave the intersection of art and nature, of the human body and the created object, the foot and the shoe, flesh and leather.

I am not one of those unhealthy fetishists who will curl up at night masturbating into a black silk slingback. I need a female presence to give life to the shoe. And I need a shoe to embellish and fully eroticize the foot.

I must admit that in all these calculations I find myself envisaging a white foot in a dark shoe, and I hope this doesn't sound racist, or more precisely I suppose "skinist." Frankly I don't see why it should. I'm talking about preference here, not prejudice. But a black-skinned foot in a dark shoe lacks contrast and tension, and the same applies to a black foot with dark painted nails. You might then think that a dark foot in a white shoe or with white painted nails might be erotic, but for me those things don't hit the pleasure centers at all.

There is one area where dark skin is infinitely more dramatic than white and that is in the matter of sperm. White strands and globs of semen standing out against the background of a taut black instep is an immensely powerful and moving image; however, it seems somehow peripheral to the true stuff of foot and shoe fetishism. It may involve a foot, but it is somehow not *about* that foot.

Rather, for me, the entire nexus of foot and shoe sexuality is emblematized by the peep-toe. Ah, the peep-toe, that most perverse and erotic element of all. The foot is partly concealed by the body of the shoe, but here at its very apex we have a small, circular, inviting orifice. The bare flesh of the big toe is indecently revealed, ready to be touched or kissed, pushing out through this hole, penis-like no doubt, mimicking penetration, glossy, vibrant, cherry red. The erotic charge of the peep-toe is more potent, exciting, and dangerous than anything I know. Catherine wore a lot of peep-toed shoes.

The question of what foot and shoe fetishists do in bed isn't a particularly complex one. Nor is it difficult to answer. They do everything that everybody else does, but they do one or two other things as well. They (we) use all the techniques and actions and positions that everyone else does, but usually the woman is wearing high heels.

The fetishist will fondle his partner's feet, of course. He will kiss them, perhaps lick and suck the toes. The woman will run her feet, whether shod or bare, over her partner's body. Of course, she will concentrate on his erogenous zones, of course she will use her feet to massage his genitals, she may well press her feet into his face.

The practice of taking your partner's toes in your mouth is known to some people as "shrimping," and in one sense this seems like rather a good term. The toes do resemble shrimps by virtue of being pink, curled, and soft, and of about the right size. But the word shrimping sounds like a frivolous and silly activity, and when I have a woman's toes in my mouth, the feeling is anything but frivolous. For me it is a moment of breathtaking, stomach-churning intensity.

In answer to a question Catherine asked right at the beginning, I was able to assure her that I had no desire to be walked on, trodden on, or kicked. There's a certain undeniable element of self-abasement involved in scrabbling around at a woman's feet, but humiliation and subjugation are no part of my own sexual profile, although I'm sure there are other foot and shoe fetishists for whom they're essential.

I think it's important to say right away that I perceive myself as a serious person. I read newspapers. I follow politics. I try to keep up with the new books and films, plays and exhibitions. In my interactions with the world, in my job (which is dull but responsible), in my tastes and opinions and beliefs, I would say that I'm a substantial and complete and serious person. Yet I can see that there is something profoundly unserious about being a foot and shoe fetishist.

Certain sexual obsessions, let us say an addiction to pain, either given or received, a taste for violation of the self or others, a compulsive attraction toward children or animals or feces, these things carry with them a sense of scale, of drama, of awful consequence, that a love of feet and shoes simply does not.

This is a paradox and occasionally a problem. Here I am, this serious person, seriously obsessed with something that most people are unable to take seriously. Tell people you are obsessed with bondage, and see them react. They may express surprise or shock or disapproval, and this expression may be real or feigned; it may be only an attempt to hide their real feelings, it may be some conditioned response, but either way there *is* a definite response. They look at you as though you're talking about something risky and edgy and, yes, serious. But tell them you're a foot fetishist and they giggle. For them, it's a joke, it's funny, it's not serious sex. Yet for me it is. For me it is the only kind of serious sex.

For a long time I wasn't sure whether I was a fetishist or a partialist. This is an important distinction. A partialist is someone who likes, who is attracted to, a nice pair of feet or shoes; he enjoys them and they add to his sexual pleasure, but they are not *necessary* for that pleasure, whereas a true fetishist needs the shoes or feet in order to derive any sexual pleasure at all. The presence of the fetish object is a necessary precondition before sexual activity can even take place.

Personally I'm quite sure that I *could* make love to a woman who had ordinary or even unattractive feet, or to a woman who was wearing dreary or ugly shoes (so in that sense it might be argued that I'm not a true fetishist at all); but why should I? The bottom line is I really don't think I could be *bothered* to make love to a woman whose feet I didn't find attractive. There are enough pairs of attractive feet and shoes in the world that you simply don't need to force yourself to make love to someone who doesn't possess them.

I didn't always feel this way. I wasn't always like this. It has been all slide and slippage, a slow ascent or descent, I'm not sure which, on some sexual escalator, or a rudderless drift downstream over treacherous waters, a path of least resistance, not that I would ever have wanted to resist.

I was once more or less orthodox in my relations with women. I went out on dates. I went to parties. I met women in the course of my work and my social life. I talked to them, went out with them, enjoyed their company, went to bed with them, had fun sometimes. It was okay, but it was rarely *more* than okay. It was usually not quite right. I never found exactly what I was looking for, because for a long time I didn't know what I was looking for, and even when I did know, there was a time when I wasn't prepared to admit it.

I had always known that I was attracted to women who had good feet. I knew I liked women who wore good shoes. But I tried to pretend that feet and shoes weren't my only interests. And to some extent that wasn't entirely a pretense. I liked women with good breasts and good legs and good minds too. These things were attractive and appealing. I could even see that they were desirable, but they were never necessary.

There was no road-to-Damascus experience about it, no crucial moment, no trauma. I simply decided to concentrate and focus. I gradually realized I'd had enough of all that relationship nonsense. I knew I couldn't go on the way I had been doing, seeing women who didn't quite hit the spot, so I decided to take the plunge. I decided to go to hell in a shoe box. I would stop pretending. I would stop being a partialist. I'd go the whole hog and throw myself into proper foot and shoe fetishism. I would stop looking for a woman with a good personality or a good complexion. I would not be averse to these things, but they would be only peripheral pleasures. Feet were what really mattered.

You might think that in doing this I had abandoned a part of my humanity, that being a fetishist involved some kind of demeaning bondage. Wrong. What I felt I had abandoned was all the dead wood, the window dressing. I was getting down to essentials, and for me it was a supreme liberation. When I met a woman, a prospective sexual partner, there would be no more conversations about what films we'd seen, what music we liked, what hopes and plans we had for the future, where we liked to spend our holidays. There would be no more worries about where the relationship was "going." All I needed was a woman with a great pair of feet. She didn't even need to have great shoes. I'd be only too happy to provide those for her.

The next step that I took is the only aspect of my obsession that ever actually made me feel ashamed. It was certainly the only thing I ever did that was even remotely illegal. I began to find ways of stealing the shoes from women's feet. Not quite literally. I didn't leap on women, knock them to the ground, and rob them. I never used violence; rather, I used a great deal of skill and cunning.

There are certain occasions, certain situations, when women take their shoes off in public. It happens in parks or at the beach, although women rarely wear very exciting shoes when they're walking on sand or shingle. They also take their shoes off in restaurants or bars, at the theater or cinema. At parties and dances, foot-sore women frequently kick off their shoes and dance in their bare or stockinged feet.

I suppose my greatest advantage in all this was that I didn't look like the sort of man who would steal women's shoes. What would such a man look like, in any case? I would saunter past my "victim," looking innocent but purposeful, as though I had many things on my mind other than women's shoes. It was surprisingly easy. In parks, the women would be sunbathing with their eyes closed, or engrossed in a book or listening to a personal stereo. In restaurants and bars, they tended to be engrossed in food, drink, and conversation. In the theater or cinema, they were watching the entertainment, although the seating arrangements here often made access very difficult. At parties and dances, the women were partying or dancing. In none of these situations were they expecting to have their shoes stolen. They would be guarding their handbags, their keys, their credit cards, but they would feel quite relaxed about their shoes. And that's when I used to pounce, swiftly, deftly, expertly. A certain amount of crawling about on the floor was often required, but that went with the territory. I stole the shoes and I was gone. Later I'd imagine the women walking home shoeless, their bare feet exposed to the common gaze, and there was a certain amount of sly pleasure in that too.

If I had taken you to my archive I would have tried to explain all this to you. Perhaps you would be looking at me a little askance by now—Catherine certainly was. But it would be time to press on. I would ask you to select a pair of shoes you liked and I would help you to put them on. You would realize that you were not the first to have worn them, that other women had been here as you were, and I would hope that the thought excited you.

We would enter the inner sanctum, the secret chamber, and I would draw the curtain closed behind us to enclose the space, the walls full of shoes, the ceiling mirrored, the floor lined with deep wool carpet. We would stand at the center and I would undress us both. Perhaps you would have chosen a pair of red leather high-heeled mules with a peep toe. I would kneel at your feet and kiss your flesh where it met the leather, then I would lay you down and fuck you long and intensely and tenderly and no doubt you would look up, look past me, up at the mirrored ceiling, at our surroundings. And undoubtedly you would look at the rows of shoes, and you might think about all the past or future perverse acts these shoes represented. And with my cock inside you, with your feet encased in shoes of your own choosing, I would hope that you would finally be coming very close to understanding me.

HELMUT NEWTON

Photographs

fet·ish (fet′ish, fē′tish), *n.* **1.** an object regarded with awe as being the embodiment or habitation of a potent spirit or as having magical potency. **2.** any object, idea, etc. eliciting unquestioning reverence, respect, or devotion: *to make a fetish of high grades.* **3.** *Psychol.* any object, part of the body, etc., that, although not of a sexual nature, causes an erotic response or fixation. Also, **fetich.** [earlier *fateish* < Pg *feitiço* charm, sorcery (*n.*), artificial (adj.) < L *facticius* FACTITIOUS; r. *fatisso, fetisso* < Pg, as above] — **fet′ish·like′,** *adj.* —**Syn. 1.** talisman, amulet.

fet·ish·ism (fet′i shiz′əm, fē′ti-), *n.* **1.** belief in or use of fetishes. **2.** *Psychiatry.* the compulsive use of some object or part of the body as a stimulus in the course of attaining sexual gratification, as a shoe, a lock of hair, underclothes, etc. **3.** blind devotion: *a fetishism of sacrifice to one's children.* Also, fetichism. [FETISH + ISM] —**fet′ish·is′tic,** *adj.*

fet·ish·ist (fet′i shist, fē′ti-), *n.* a person who uses fetishes. Also, **fetichist.** [FETISH + IST]

Random House Dictionary

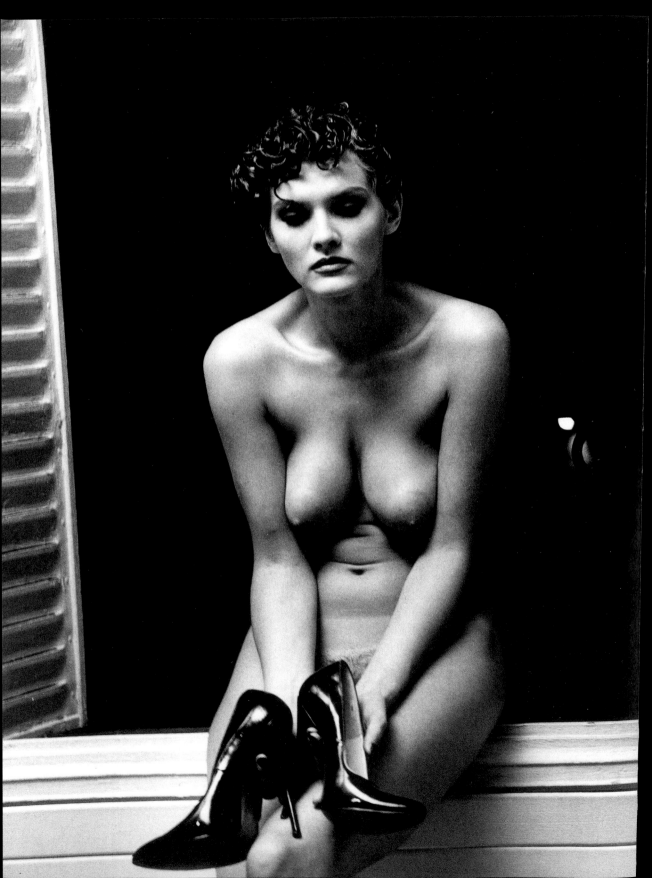

Personal Articles

(An Inventory of Bougainville's Night Case)

He was walking in the street.
He wished that he might suddenly be transplanted
into a bath of vice (scenery and action).
He was prepared to pay to gain entry to a vicious ambiance,
but the porno theater looked seedy . . .

The Comb

The comb is a piece of ivory or shell, of horn, at one time more crudely made by inserting spikes into a wooden handle, which is used to smooth the hair, to separate it into distinct masses on either side of a part, which reveals the roots of the hair, the whiter hide of the skull. The comb becomes a useless, purely nostalgic object for bald men, who generally have the ebonite melted down or else store it in safekeeping, like a relic, a souvenir of a happy and fertile period. The comb is then placed in a small case that precisely sheathes each tooth. If bald men attach such great importance to preserving the teeth of the comb, it is because they look upon the breaking of a tooth as a harbinger of something far worse than baldness.

The Cotton Swab

The cotton swab, which is used to extract from the ear's inner cavity those unctuous, yellow, waxy secretions known as cerumen, is a small wooden stick around the end of which a small quantity of cotton has been wrapped. Cotton swabs are sold in boxes of a hundred in pharmacies and supermarkets. However, some families demonstrate the pointlessness, the purely luxurious nature, of such a purchase by making their own cotton swabs out of a broken match-stick or a lollipop stick, one end of which is carefully whittled with a knife so that the cotton can be attached to the wood. The patented Q-Tip and the homemade cotton swab serve essentially the same purpose, which is to cleanse the ears, and can, through repeated rubbing, produce the same pleasant irritation of the tissues of the auricular labyrinth or even, in children, small spasms, if one pushes them into the still unexplored channels next to the fibrous and translucent membrane that transmits sound, or if the manipulation is particularly adroit. Certain women also use cotton swabs soaked in alcohol to cleanse their children's navels, or soaked in solvent to remove nail-polish stains from their skin when they paint their nails. Some people claim that the use of cotton swabs is harmful: not only is there a danger of piercing the eardrum, but the swab can force the auricular excrement into inaccessible passageways, thereby giving rise to small eruptions that may harden irrevocably to the point where they totally fill and block the passage connecting the middle to the inner ear, thus precluding forever any further apprehension of sound. Instead of cotton swabs, our great-grandmothers simply used the bare, thin metal of their hairpins.

The Cat-o'-Nine-Tails

The cat-o'-nine-tails hangs among the dust brushes from ceiling hooks in the dark back room of the hardware store. It envelops, within its stationary straps, the cries of battered children; it exhales the pleasures of lovers gone astray.

The Ether Mask

Disassembled and empty, with some parts wrapped in tissue paper and the bulb, nosepiece, horn, and central portion, a ball of rubber or tin, stored separately in a wooden box, the ether mask grimly awaits its moment in the glass case of the ear, nose, and throat specialist. Intended to replace more complex anesthetic techniques involving laudanum or mandrake, the ether mask originally consisted of a silver housing into which one placed a sponge soaked in ether, which housing was connected by a tube to an inhaler, a mask that slipped under the lips and fit tightly against the gums of the child, who was instructed to bite down on it while his nose was clamped with a small metal device to prevent nasal breathing and force him to inhale anesthetic vapors to the point of complete narcosis (the ether mask was frequently used for operations on the tonsils and for circumcisions). The ether mask perfected by Dr. Ombredanne in 1932 consisted of a steel or rubber vessel, a mask that covered the entire face (although the child was advised to breathe only through the mouth in order to prevent too much dulling of the brain), and a small bulb that the child himself pressed to propel the vapors of ether until he succumbed, inert, in the operating chair. This form of anesthesia induced only partial loss of consciousness: the child was perfectly aware of the scissors being introduced into his throat and of the blood that suddenly filled his mouth. The ether subsequently induced vomiting and nightmares that engraved themselves forever in memory. Few ether addicts own an ether mask, though it could greatly facilitate their inhalations. They prefer to breathe the ether directly from a flask or else to drink it. The ether mask is also not recommended as a cure for insomnia or for brief bouts of depression. The mere description of it, provided it contains a sufficient surfeit of detail, has been known to put readers to sleep.

The Neck Brace

The neck brace is a leather bandage with holes in it, a casing with steel fasteners like those of a trunk, which molds itself exactly to the nape and neck, in some cases down to the shoulders, and supports the jaw when vertebration is absent, when the cylinder of the neck, circular splint is generally pierced, as if by loopholes, to allow air in, obviously, but also to allow a tongue or a dagger to pass through, for young people afflicted with this congenital weakness eagerly seek such contact with the rosiness of the papillaries or with cold steel.

And when night falls and one opens the precious casing, previously hidden by a knot or a chest thrust out so high as to betray the rigidity of the face or the fixedness of the regard, one has to take the head in one's hands, and swathing it in linen—for it slips, it twists, it falls back—take the mouth, freed at last and driveling, and do with it as one wishes; the blood that surges from the heart comes to a halt in one of many nexuses, the protruding little muscular callosity that they say marks masculinity runs on without stopping, like a machine, and the subject dies of exhaustion: he will suffocate if one leaves him in the void, if one does not hold him up on either side, between one's palms, like the rarest of illuminated books.

The Static Electricity Machine

Originally it was noticed that yellow amber, if rubbed, attracted light, dry substances. People explained this by saying that the rubbing gave the amber a soul and this soul attracted light substances as with a gentle wind. Then a learned man by the name of William Gilbert noticed that the property of attracting light substances after rubbing was common to jade, diamond, sapphire, ruby, opal, amethyst, aquamarine, quartz, sulfur, mastic, resin, arsenic, talc, and still other compounds. Moreover, he found that these compounds attracted not only bits of straw but also wood, metal leaf and filings, stones, various kinds of earth, and even liquids such as water and oil. But the honor of constructing the first electricity machine from a ball of sulfur belongs to Otto von Guericke, the burgermeister of Magdeburg: "Take a bowl of copper, or as it is called, a phial, the thickness of a child's head; fill it with sulfur crushed in a mortar, and heat over a fire to melt the sulfur, which must then be stored in a dry place. Next, pierce this globe in such a way as to pass an iron rod through it along its axis. . . . " With this rudimentary machine, Otto von Guericke, working in the dark, was able to observe the luminous phenomenon that accompanies the rubbing of the sulfur globe, that is, the electrical spark. The light that he obtained was very weak, exactly comparable, in his own words, to the phosphorescence observed when sugar is ground in a dark room. In order to hear the crackling of the spark, one has to place one's ear very close to the globe. In the attractions and repulsions that the sulfur globe exerted on light substances placed in its vicinity, von Guericke thought he discerned phenomena analogous to the attractions and repulsions that the terrestrial globe exerts on bodies placed within its sphere of influence.

The English physicist Grey was the first to electrify the human body. He discovered that if one places a child in a horizontal position on ribbons of horsehair, and if one then places a rubbed glass tube in contact with the child, the patient's feet will attract light substances. The Frenchman Du Fay established a distinction between two kinds of electricity: vitreous electricity and resinous electricity. The former refers to the electricity of glass, quartz, precious gems, animal hairs, and wool. The latter refers to that of amber, copal gum, lacquer, silk, thread, and paper. Each kind of electricity attracts electricities of the other kind and repels electricities of its own kind. In an experiment that elicited universal enthusiasm, Du Fay drew electric sparks from the human body. He first attached silk cords to the ceiling of his study for insulation and then, after lying down on a small platform suspended from those cords, had himself electrified through contact with a large rubbed glass tube. If one then placed one's finger close to the patient's body, a spark leapt from the body to the finger. In the darkness one could make out a luminous emanation.

Hausen, a professor at Leipzig, built a machine whose design appeared in a work published in Paris in 1748, William Watson's *Expériences et observations sur l'électricité*. A young abbé turned a crank that set a glass sphere in motion. The role of the conductor was filled by a child suspended in the air by means of silk cords, which insulated him. Through his feet the child collected the electricity developed by the surface of the sphere. The current flowed along his body and was transmitted through his right hand to a little girl seated on a cake of resin. The girl offered her left hand to the patient and then used her electrified right hand to attract gold leaf from a nearby insulated table.

Finally, in 1768, the English optician Ramsden made one final improvement to the machines then in use: instead of the glass cylinder, he used a flat glass plate rotating between four layers of hide stuffed with horsehair and pressed against the glass by a spring. It is interesting to note that the reason for replacing the glass sphere by a cylinder or disk was that the spheres had given rise to a considerable number of accidents: they exploded suddenly and showered the experimenters with dangerous shards. The disks sometimes

broke in two while filling with electrical current, but at least they did
not explode, and their use was safe. With these machines people
succeeded in simulating a rain of fire with water flowing in an electrified fountain. They also produced shooting stars from a rapidly
rotating metal disc equipped with points at intervals equidistant
from the center.

But of all the phenomena discovered at this time, the one that
aroused the most curiosity and impressed the imagination most
deeply was the use of electrical sparks to ignite combustible
material. Dr. Ludolf, of Berlin, ignited ether with sparks from an
electrified glass tube. By drawing sparks with his finger, Winckler, in
Leipzig, ignited not only ether but also *eau-de-vie*, oxhorn extract,
and other spirituous liquors. Watson, in England, repeated and
extended these experiments. In addition to *eau-de-vie* of varying
concentrations, he ignited various liquids containing volatile oils,
such as spirit of lavender, spirit of dulcified saltpeter, peony water,
elixirs and styptics, and essence of terebinth, lemon, orange, juniper,
and sassafras.

In the novel *Pauliska ou la Perversité moderne*, published in 1796,
Reveroni Saint-Cyr teaches us how to liquefy the breath of pretty
women, how love, like rabies, can be inoculated through a bite, and
how, by rubbing the flesh of children or women, one can obtain a
rejuvenating magnetic source.... And on a parchment in red letters:

> *Love is a form of rabies; it can be inoculated like this disease through
> a bite (method). Calcified turtledove bones, camphor, and snake skin
> (operations). Repeated bites.*

> *Love being the physical union of two beings so that the masses of
> both become commingled, one must give impetus to the atoms.
> Irritate the fibers with ash from the hair and eyebrows of the
> operator. Powerful inspiration through the pores; extensive rubbing
> of the skin. For drink, the operator may use his liquefied breath.*

The Vacuum Machine

Consisting of a bell jar set atop a finely crafted table and connected
by a system of pumps, pipes, and wheels through which the air removed from the chamber could be evacuated, the vacuum machine
was inexorable in the sense that it created an unreal space, devoid of

all particles and impossible for any sentient object to live in. In demonstrations of comparative physics this machine became a parlor game: a live bird was placed underneath the bell jar, which was then sealed, with care to make sure that the rubber gaskets and washers intended to ensure an airtight fit were all in place. The bird would flutter in a panic around the glass cage, to which the glaucous eyes of the participants were glued, but when the physicist's flesh-less, acid-eaten hand set the wheels in motion and the air, propelled by the pump, began to thin, the bird would cease to float in this weightless space; no longer able to fly, it would immediately flatten itself against the marquetry, its heart and the little ivory marbles of its eyes would explode, its fragile breastbone would crumple, and the bell jar could then be lifted with a whistle of decompression to remove a small powdery, bony, feathery, and slightly moist mass.

If one enlarged the chamber to create a human-sized vacuum and operated the pneumatic system after placing a naked, blind-folded man inside, the same process would take place. The flesh would immediately turn blue, and the man would be crushed, riveted in place by the mass of the void; all the flesh of the surface of his face and of his body would explode, as if eaten away by a violent jet of acid, and soon nothing would remain but his skeleton, like a hawthorn heated white-hot.

Translated from the French by Arthur Goldhammer

The chapters above are excerpted from Hervé Guibert's collection Vice, © *J. Bertoin, 1991/Balland.*

The Respectful Fetishist

I

At the age of eleven or so, I loved to sweep downstairs and into the drawing room in a long dress. I suppose, had I been less wrapped up in my own self-presentation, I'd have sensed that, as the novels say, "the unease in the room was palpable." My parents said nothing, or brightly congratulated me on my stylish appearance.

The fancy dress chest up in the nursery was crammed with sailor suits, military uniforms, brocaded cloaks lined with pale blue damask, Victorian dresses, petticoats, and assorted shoes. How many little boys, in how many nurseries, on their knees and burrowing deep into such fancy dress chests, have intoxicated themselves on the erotic aromas of slightly damp silks amid mothballs?

There was another chest, a black tin one, in my father's study, which contained Marxist texts. The idea was that visitors, already on the lookout for secret radio transmitters picking up the instructions from Moscow that had been beamed to our Irish home, should not trip over copies of *Capital* or the works of Vladimir. That chest, too, I would open and peer into, though not with the same sensuous abandon.

II

In the end, though not when I was eleven, I read Marx, and in Part Four of Chapter One of *Capital*, came upon the old boy's reflections on commodity fetishism, and his claim that "the mysterious character of the commodity-form consists ... simply in the fact that the commodity reflects the social characteristics of men's own labor as objective characteristics of the products of labor themselves ... Through this substitution, the products of labor become commodities, sensuous things which are at the same time suprasensible or social."

Maybe sensing that he might not have carried the audience with him on this one, Karl took another crack at the idea: ". . . to find an analogy we must take flight into the misty realm of religion. There the products of the human brain appear as autonomous figures endowed with a life of their own, which enter into relations both with each other and with the human race. So it is in the world of commodities with the products of men's hands. I call this the fetishism which attaches itself to the products of labor as soon as they are produced as commodities, and is therefore inseparable from the production of commodities."

In other words, the gauzy stockings which end up crammed against the schoolboy's nose represent the congealed labor of the stocking weaver, and the exploitative conditions imposed on the stocking weaver by the stocking manufacturer. Of course, the surplus value extorted from our poor stocking weaver pays not only for the master's Rolls-Royce, but also for the Benetton ad enjoining stocking purchasers to remember Third World oppression, even as the delightful model becomes the fetish object representing the stockings and vice versa.

III

Near the village of Ardmore, up the southern Irish coast from the house in which I grew up, and occasionally patrolled in Victorian lady's rig, was a wishing well called St. Declan's Well. You were allowed to make one wish a year, taking a white stone out of the pool and keeping it for the twelve-month period while St. Declan, other duties permitting, worked his way down the wish list. Before St. Declan came along, mooring his coracle at the Ardmore rocks in the fifth century, it had been a Druid well. People had made their wishes in the same old way, and either then, or in the Declan phase, they had started leaving bits of rag or clothing on the bushes around the well, presumably as a reminder to the Druids or saint that their wish was on file. As St. Declan's recuperative powers grew in repute, a brisk trade in relics arose. Pieces of wood were sold as supposed remnants of his coracle. Statues of Declan reposed in the churches.

Other saints across Europe were prompting the same business and the Portuguese called these relics, rosaries, and images *feitiços*, or charms. The first Portuguese missionaries who went to West Africa noted the wooden figures and stones which served as the temporary residence of gods or spirits there. The natives regarded as deeply vulgar the idea that these objects were, in and of themselves, sacred. But concealing their true relationship to the spirits from the importunate missionaries, they made a great show of agreeing with the foreigners' foolish idea that the objects themselves had intrinsic magical or spiritual qualities. The missionaries seized the objects, denounced them as idolatrous, but did not destroy them, and took them back to Europe where they ended up in museums. In English they were called fetishes; and indeed, I suppose you could call the missionaries' respect a form of commodity fetishism.

Fetishism was born, and experienced an exciting sex life in late-nineteenth-century decadent and early-twentieth-century avant-garde circles, where the primary project, in the words of Peter Wollen in *Raiding the Icebox*, was "the technical realization of the ideal object of masculine desire.... In the twentieth century, this project reached a point of delirium with two modern artists, Kokoschka and Bellmer, both of whom had dolls manufactured for their personal gratification. Kokoschka took his (a life-sized replica of his ex-lover, made by her dressmaker, Hermine Moos) for excursions in his carriage, for meals in restaurants, where he insisted that a place be laid for her, and to the theater where she sat in the seat next to his. Bellmer, who knew of Kokoschka's doll, crafted a whole series of dolls, which he arranged in provocative postures and photographed. They became famous after they were publicized as 'surrealist objects' in the magazine *Minotaure*, and were later categorized as 'bachelor machines.'"

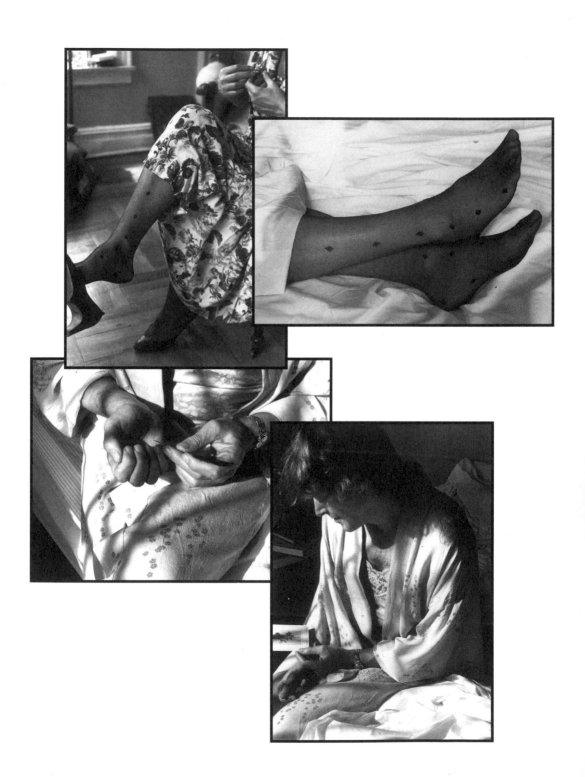

From this baroque (and, if the truth be told, rather vulgar) fetishism, it was downhill all the way, to the fourth edition of the *Diagnostic and Statistical Manual of Mental Disorders* (The American Psychiatric Association, 1994), bible of shrinks, clinicians, expert witnesses, and insurance companies. Its entry 302.81, on fetishism, describes it this way: "The paraphiliac focus in Fetishism involves the use of nonliving objects (the 'fetishes'). Among the more common fetish objects are women's underpants, bras, stockings, shoes, boots, or other wearing apparel.... Usually the Paraphilia begins by adolescence, although the fetish may have been endowed with special significance earlier in childhood. Once established, Fetishism tends to be chronic."

Since the *DSM* is a manual, it must provide "diagnostic criteria" convincing to insurance companies: "A. Over a period of at least six months, recurrent, intense, sexually arousing fantasies, sexual urges, or behaviors involving the use of nonliving objects (e.g. female undergarments). B. The fantasies, sexual urges, or behaviors cause clinically significant distress or impairment in social, occupational, or other important areas of functioning ... "

Another entry, 302.3, addresses "Transvestic Fetishism," and concludes with the thought that, "In some individuals the motivation for cross-dressing may change over time, temporarily or permanently, with sexual arousal in response to cross-dressing diminishing or disappearing. In such instances, the cross-dressing becomes an antidote to anxiety or depression or contributes to a sense of peace or calm."

IV

A sense of peace or calm is exactly the effect I was after, slipping into J.'s dress and adjusting her dear little shoe just so.

The old cross-dressing urge had stayed dormant since those sessions with the dress-up chest, although, between the ages of fourteen and eighteen, I did wear a kilt every Sunday at my Scottish school, naturally preferring this garb to the herring-bone tweed suit which was a permitted option on the Sabbath. But it had come up in connection with the hyperbolic challenge of a magazine editor who said that she would wear a dress if she saw me in one. No need to issue that challenge twice.

The plan, to be expressed through the medium of my 1940s Leica, wielded by J., was to dissociate cross-dressing from the hectic modalities of "drag" and reassociate it with the dignity and repose of Victorian fetishism, where the objects—stocking, skirt, silk dressing gown, slip, hands, card suggesting *temps perdu*—would be allowed to speak calmly and peacefully for themselves. As representations of the feminine, in contrast to the insulting parodism of drag, I suppose you could call them photographs of a respectful fetishist.

Fetishism, after all, is not so far removed from animism, for which I've always had a *tendresse*. Animism is a great respecter of objects.

Later I proudly showed the photographs to one of my neighbors, a carpenter who was a keen reader of *Soldier of Fortune*. Word of the photographs quickly spread around the Adobe, a rough motel where I was living at the time, in Aptos, on California's central coast. Soon I had only to appear on the outside stairway from my upper suite of rooms for mothers to cry for their little ones and rush them indoors.

V

St. Declan's Well is on land that went with my mother's house, now owned by myself and my brothers. Every now and then, we worry that the percentage of white stones in the well is inevitably diminishing, as the well-wishers carry them off in their pockets. Should we chuck in a new bucket of white stones every couple of years and chalk it up to Fetish Upkeep? Somehow we never do, and the stones never entirely run out.

Coriolan

D o I have to house myself in this bone? Coming as I do from far away, the bone is too small at first. Too small, but it grows. It grows. Now I have a long domed thighbone and my home is in it. Finger bone as it might have been, neither head bone nor kneecap, it is a long hollow, snappable as a celery stick, a fish bone, a dead man's bone. Having lived around it or, like a dog, dug it up, you know not where it came from, yet dare not breathe on it.

Inside the bone, there is room. A large room opens in the bone, more room, more. The bone encloses light, yet the light flows through the room. Where from? I have come through a little door and am astonished, as I straighten up, to recognize, all around this oval room of illuminated bone, such windows: are they peepholes? Not even perpendicular frames into which smaller frames of steel snugly fit. Not even the mircd glass oblong in the rain-ringed plaster of an attic ceiling, the trap you have to shove aloft with a rusty rod. No: here the windows are perennially open, huge flute holes through which winds blow their tunes.

Well, so, seeing such windows, should I run, shaking with fright, to close them? Instead, I run to look out: and there is the town. Through it a blue-green river flows. I see beside it, far off, an isosceles silhouette. No mistake: a fisherman is standing there. Just then he hooks a shining fish, shining and curly, scaly, striped. He stares up at the window I am standing in. We connect, at an angle, midway along the fishless line between our looks. Then I know I am invited. In his fist, his left fist, he holds an oar, upright; it is not a winnowing fan. An open fire, he hears it crackling beside him, on the shore of this river.

But the room—I had to be in the bone room. What are these coral streaks in the whiteness I am standing on? And these other windows: I float to the next one. Look out—see a country of dense forest, caverns, ravines with familiar tombs carved into towering scarps. Sparkling far off, an ocean. A few white whisks of cloud over there mean that the simoon has come and gone.

So these columns, orange trees in the gardens, walled shadowy lanes, wisps of smoke that rise from holes in tiled roofs, cluster on either side of the river, and the river runs freely to the ocean. Except for the tinkle of goat bells from below, the room is silent and, wait a moment, the splashed coral reminds me of bloods I have seen elsewhere, and then there was no such hush.

Looking out again I hear the single note of a watchman's horn. What pleasure, ah, the pang of it, to smell the animals. Goat and cow, wild pig, the ferret who smells of hay rotting in the sun, the spoiled-fruit reek of a puma. I begin to hear voices, now some are murmuring, now some crack into muted sobs, screams without rage, yet the room—open windows, flute breath, and all—is far away from all that, and it is clean.

With slow steps, somehow, and between my sharp shoulder blades beaten down, bent double by sorrow, jaw tightening, lips stretched, neck tendons tight, I cross the floor, drawn to a table. There is a table, made of alabaster, or marble, or crystallized bone.

As I approach it, I see that the table gives off a glow that I have seen before. It is the white cube of rock, veined with red, I saw long ago in an arroyo forking from the north into the Rio Grande, half a day's ride west of Langtry. It is a natural table, on a ledge; rock shelters, once deep, had been shallowed by time, by weather. This is my table, and it is calling to me. Here, with the light falling on the table from the window beyond it, I will be at work, working at what?—and forever? Off and on—always the view to spark interest. I tell myself that the fisherman, and there he is again, it is Steve Goddard, the mackerel catcher of Cadgwith, will show me, above and below ground, the people in Coriolan, this lost city I despaired ever to find.

In the taverns and kitchens, there will be people; secret pastures will open to us when we unlatch gates that are intangible in the depth of time.

I am looking up, the far ravines, the forest, the ocean have not yet gone away, but all at once I am peering down at the surface of this bone rock table. Here is a golden fish, under a coating that took thousands of years to become hard, yet not opaque. Snail-paced sedimentation on luminous bone; powdered under the pressure of an unknowing that sustains every individual time bubble (each with its own tension, its own air, its own inscrutable vacancy), a substance has been sieved to lacquer the table, to trap the fish. One bright round eye is fastened on me: this fish, clothed in a brocade of curly glittering scales, itching to wiggle, is alive. I am ready, with this knife in my belt, to attack the bone surface, assail the lacquered rock, set the fish free.

Then, in the bone, a script appears, also coated, at first a script written by a child, in separate crude letters, coated as if fluid but crystallizing light had for a long time washed back and forth across it building the layers of rock or of bone, while it constituted impetuously, too, the letters, which keep changing, so that the legend changes its code every time you look, the characters themselves changing, now Coptic, now Latin, now Georgian, now Arabic, Armenian, Greek, more and more certain the strokes, less and less decipherable their legend, on account of the mutations. No way, opening eyes or narrowing them, to arrest the flux of the script. Whoever is writing it, the legend, though it is no lengthier than a breath, forbids me to think it a message for me.

What is this? And who is this onlooker, who does not know if he is being fooled, thwarted, or waved away?

Surely another glimpse from the other window will break this trance the script has put me in. —Goddard is there, he beckons, beckons again urgently, our eyebeams are knit once more, and now he has placed his fish on a grill over his fire. How can he have survived the sixty-odd years, the wars, the stupor of our country? From his painted boat, out at sea, feeling the tug, whenever fish lips took his hook, pass from the end of the line into his finger, he might have caught a thousand shoals of mackerel. Inland now, he won't mind waiting. Didn't they say that waiting is three-fourths of a fisherman's occupation?

I cup my hands to my mouth and shout: "Hodié yok!" There is no echo, because there is no sound, and now not the script, which is extinguished, but the scarps are moving with their tombs, moving to encircle the town, or not quite—still there is a gap, to my left, through which daylight has carved a crevasse and I could slip. Can I find the door and crouch and worm my way through, then run for the crevasse? I know the circle has closed. Even if I could find the little bone door, what's the use? I have lost the knack of effort, am bereft of the vigilance any least effort used to bring. The fury I contained, to keep my eyes open, their motion constant, has left me. The follies, calamities, the partings that broke my sleep, of them no trace by which to measure this drifting off, nothing to hold me through this letting go.

Bondage
in
Black and White

223

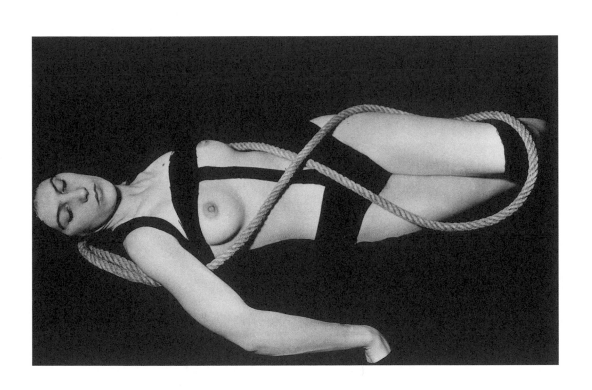

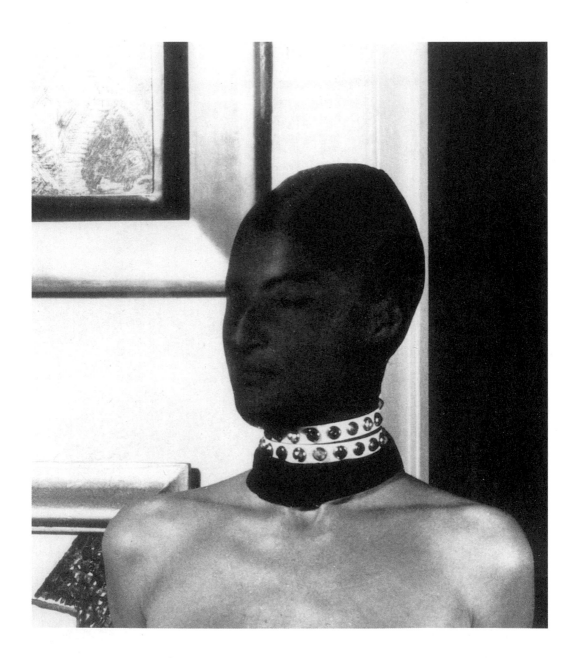

Returning the Book of Common Prayer to the Library in Order to Check Out the Marquis de Sade

1.

If any arise, disoriented,
And the world like a working field
Held out, holding baby formula, ceremoniously.
I can't believe what they're doing to each other.
What devotion toward the hard, striking branches in the rain.
"Let us worship and fall down."
Grandiloquent fever, as we stand and surrender
To the slovenly leaves, eat the rose wildly and vanish,
Like crosses when he comes climbing out of God's mouth,
And came to be what they claimed at once.
What can't be had in the moment as it opens up?
"But lay up treasure for yourselves," preserve the farm,
Pass out from beyond all understanding, evermore
a ruler.

2.

I've seen the way people climb out of themselves
And onto the thorns, looking for a way of not knowing
What to expect, and to make it beautiful.
To think of themselves as buried treasure
And to say: "I treasure you."
What is it that makes the pine (the spine) fly?

Red peppers and the fisted sun.
A silver tree that came onto the morning sky.
We want to be whole.
We've gone down to the basement with our applications.

Syringes and these gentle horses bite the sweet ground.
So the miracle chain.
So it be discreet in the severity of its doing.
So it makes you feel like nothing is ever going to change.

3.

Science fiction clouds against a slaughtering sky
Coming at you and blown up in a critical attire.

It was you who conceived the project we found ourselves in
Like a box-office smash in the sunlight.

We came wearing our names backward to carry off the silver tree.
Then in the refined cell, sinking.

ANDRÉ ALEXIS

The Third Terrace

La main est l'un des animaux de l'homme...

Francis Ponge

I was born in Ottawa in 1957. My family was middle-class. That is, my parents had raised themselves from the gutter and hoped to get even further from it through their children. To that end, I was given a good education. After high school I went to the University of Ottawa, where I studied Literature for a term and then Art History.

As far as I can recall, I was unexceptional in every way. I was plump and socially graceless. My mind had only two speeds: Dead Slow and Stop. (I did have beautiful hands, but I wasn't especially proud of them. Most of the time, I wore loose-fitting gloves.)

When I graduated I discovered that I was ill-equipped for the world. Being able to tell Bosch from Brueghel doesn't open many doors, and I wasn't always able to do even that much. So, with the grudging support of my parents, I decided to become an artist.

I had only one influence: Piero della Francesca. It was Piero this and Piero that. I lived, ate, and shat Renaissance perspective. (Not that I ever mastered it. Most of my canvases ended up black from the false lines I drew on them, but I persevered.)

After a year of devotion to painting, I had become somewhat
more adept, but I was way out of step with the Art of my time. I did
exhibit two of my "blackened" della Francescas in a school gymnasium,
and for a second there I was almost popular. An art critic called me
a "bleak ironist," and that gave my reputation a little fillip. Still, the
Ottawa Citizen doesn't carry much weight, and, in the end, my father
bought both of my paintings after haggling about the price.

Indigent, and unwilling to return home, I put painting aside two
years after I'd taken it up. And so it was that, at twenty-five, I went to
work at the Café Wim.

It was there that I met Mr. Kingsley.

It was a Saturday in June of 1982 and I wasn't wearing gloves. Mr.
Kingsley sat by the bow window and ate his cheese on rusk. We spoke
briefly about the weather, the stink of the canal, and the state of the
federation: the usual things between diner and waiter. When he got
up to leave, however, he casually mentioned that he found my hands
attractive. He asked if I had ever thought of working in film.

Now, as he had mentioned my hands, I knew what kind of "film"
he had in mind. I had been to Hull and I had seen a few erotic
movies. (I'd even enjoyed them, without taking them too seriously.)
Still, I said yes, and he put his business card face up on the table
between us:

Mr. Charles Kingsley
White Films Production Co.
58 Denison Avenue,
Toronto, Ontario

"If you can get the money together," he said, "come see me in
Toronto."

I don't remember what impressed me most about Mr. Kingsley.
His courtesy? His business card? His natty, blue suit? It was all very appealing. I remember thinking that, with a few dollars in my pocket,
I'd be able to afford the things I needed for my art: paint and canvas, brushes and turpentine.

"Does it pay well?" I asked.

"Of course," he said.

And that was it. I would make a few erotic films and then retire
to my true calling.

I hadn't managed to save a lot of money, but I had enough for a round-trip ticket to Toronto. Moreover, I was so confident of success that I left my job at Wim's, packed my belongings in a suitcase, put my paintings in storage, and lit out for the city. There was even music in my head as I rode the bus: *East St. Louis Toodleoo.*

I arrived in Toronto on a Friday afternoon and went directly to the offices of White Films. I asked for Mr. Kingsley, but Mr. Kingsley was not in. Instead, I was taken to Mr. Bultmann, ushered into his office, suitcase and all.

"Just put your hands up on the desk, will you?" he said.

When I did, his face turned beet-red, and he began to perspire.

"I think you'll be wonderful," he said.

He looked away, pushed the papers on his desk aside, and took a Kleenex from a brightly colored box.

"We've got a little something planned. Can you start this evening?"

"Of course."

"Good. Have you got a place to stay? I mean until then . . . Are you set up?"

"I just got in. I guess I could walk around until six . . ."

"Don't have to walk around at all," he said. "Stay here. Just throw your suitcase in the corner and relax."

He wasn't an intimidating man. Short, bespectacled, and clothed in polyester is what he was. An arc of neatly trimmed red hair framed the liver spots on his pate, and he rubbed the top of his ear with the Kleenex.

"I think I'll walk around," I said.

It was my first experience of Toronto, and I couldn't help but think of it in terms of fabric, the tons of cloth it took to keep so many men and women swaddled. The clouds were flocculent, the leaves linen, and the streets seemed to unfurl.

At six o'clock I returned to Mr. Bultmann's office. Mr. Bultmann was there to meet me. With him was Thomas Merton (better known as Dick Clump), the director of what was to be my first loop.

"You feeling okay?" said Mr. Bultmann. "You don't want to rest up a little? Wash your hands? It could help put you in the mood. You got to watch the psychology thing . . . in my experience . . ."

Mr. Merton silently appraised my claws.

"Course, we don't shoot here," Mr. Bultmann continued. "Here's strictly business. You're going to King Street. That's where the action is.... You know, I really envy the young ... I'd have the stuff if I was younger, don't you think?"

He pulled his hands from their burrows. They were wrinkled, spotted, and covered in moles. Mr. Merton looked away and coughed.

T he loop was a thing called *The Master's Larder* and it lasted twenty minutes. I was costumed in black, plague-era robes. The only parts of my body clearly visible were my hands.

I played a manservant who, when the Lord and Lady of the house have gone, picks the lock of the kitchen larder. Inside, there are jars of tangerine honey and piles of bone-white, brushed-cotton tablecloths. For twenty minutes I dipped my hands in honey and pulled the cloths from their hardwood shelves, and then folded them again, meticulously.

Because this was the first time I had done anything so explicit for the camera, there were only two others present: the cameraman and the director. Mr. Merton gave me careful instructions as we filmed:

"Put your fingers in that top fold. That's it ... let them linger. Now, pull them out slowly. That's it. Slower ... crumple it a little. A little more. Crumple it. Now hold it in your knuckles. Pull it through. Slowly ... slowly."

And that's how I made my first erotic film.

A ll of this must seem incredible to those of you who don't know the industry. It was certainly incredible to me. I was being paid to reveal my hands and fingers, as well as something I had no idea I possessed: my "erotic nature."

Now, where had this "nature" come from? Where had it been hidden? How had strangers like Kingsley, Bultmann, and Merton detected it so easily? It took me a full year to discover the reality of its existence, and the discovery itself was something of an accident.

I was filming my first feature, *Sheets in Acquaba*. The story was minimal, as they usually are. In this one, Lawrence of Arabia, played by Mark Lombardo, has various erotic adventures in the Middle East. I played Berty, Lawrence's close friend, and during the first half hour I am captured by angry Arabs, beaten, and left for dead in the desert. There, I am rescued by Fatima, a wife of the Sultan. She smuggles me into the Sultan's harem, wraps me in red robes, and nurses me back to health. Our first sex scene has us choosing the bolt of cloth that would be used for my disguise. Our hands linger in the folds of yellow silk, and then I am rescued by Lawrence.

As I said, I was not yet aware of my "nature." I was professional. My hands and fingers belonged to other people: the producer, the director, whomever. But, during this scene with Fatima and Lawrence, I began to feel a strange excitement. There was something about Mark Lombardo's fingers. They were graceful, thin, and pale, but one of the joints of his left index finger had been broken, and this finger curved slightly to one side no matter how he held it. For the first time, I was captivated by the beauty of an actor's hands.

At that moment I understood what these films were all about. I saw what it was Kingsley had seen in me, and I knew why I had come to Toronto: I had been guided from below.

Naturally, I began to struggle against myself. After *Acquaba* I spent all my money on reams of canvas, pots of Gesso, and tube after tube of Winsor-Newtons. I began to paint again, passionately, though instead of returning to della Francesca I immersed myself in Neo-Expressionism. (Now, it was Mimmo Paladino I wanted, and the portraits I did were so thick the paint fell off in clumps as it dried.) I did everything I could to serve my "higher calling," as if that might protect me from the intrusion of my sexual nature.

Then, while filming *Three Sheets to the Wind*, I had my first orgasm on screen.

I'm not sure what happened. *Three Sheets* was no different from any of the other films I'd done. It was set on a pirate ship, the *Blue Flame*, and I played an Englishman captured by the buccaneers.

The pirates confine me and the two young women who are my daughters to a dreary cabin below deck. In the cabin there is a hard, unmattressed bed, a wobbly wooden table, and, on a wall, a tattered map of the seas. My daughters help me undress to my nightshirt. Then, I help them undress to their shifts and stays. Finally, I cover them with a damp, moth-eaten blanket.

The women in this scene, Molly Brand and Irene Buttress, had exquisite hands. Molly's fingers were short and thick, with long nails that she kept carefully trimmed and red as poppies. The lines on her palms were deep and rust-brown. Irene's hands were delicate, almost tiny. Her palms were white, smooth as a porcelain bowl. Together, the women unbuttoned my vest, slipping the pearl circles carefully through the woven eyes.

The sound of their hands in the fabric, the light of the candles on the table, the smell of the wool: it was all too much for me. I shivered like a Mexican hairless, and then I came.

I understand how sordid this must sound, but it has happened to everyone at some time. The cameras were stopped. The actors waited as I cleaned myself. The director said, "Take it from the un-buttoning."

And we went on as though nothing had happened.

Something *had* happened. I had gone over to the other side.

After that, I could not stop thinking of fingers and fabric. I was fascinated by them. In the morning, before work, I would stare at my palms and fingers. I imagined myself in minor accidents in which my fingers were crushed beneath the wheels of a car or shopping cart. I saw my fingers penetrating tight places: a closed flower, a moist underarm, a hole in dry, white plaster, a brass socket.

Then, about a month after *Three Sheets to the Wind*, I began to have sex with the prostitutes on Church Street. It was with them that I first experienced the joy of linseed and cotton, burlap and Vaseline.

My first encounter with a prostitute was so squalid, it's a wonder I ever went back. It was night and I was walking along Church near Carleton Street. It was raining hard, but as I passed the offices of CBC a young man, his body almost completely hidden in white silk, asked me if I was lonely. I said I was a little lonely and he pushed one of his hands out from the silk sleeves. It was his left hand, and he was missing two fingers. One, the index, was cut off at the first joint. The other, the ring, was a lovely stump, cut off just above the knuckle. They were both old injuries. Flesh had grown over the bone. I was captivated. I asked how much. Fifty dollars for silk, a hundred dollars for cotton in linseed, and two hundred dollars for oiled burlap. Having settled on burlap, we hailed a cab and went to what looked like a flophouse, on Dundas Street. I paid the desk clerk twenty-five dollars for the room.

The room itself was small and windowless. A tiny bathroom, little more than a sink beneath a mirror, was off to one side. A narrow door in one of the walls hid a small closet in which there were heaps of fabric and tubs of liquid. I stood in the center of the room as he pulled out a bolt of dry burlap that smelled of peat. So far, so good.

The problem was he was businesslike. Everything went by quickly. After I paid him, he allowed me only a brief look at his hands. (His "good" hand was unexceptional.) He rubbed them over his robe as though he were cold, perfunctorily turning them this way and that. Then he unbuckled my pants and yanked them down. I had to take down my own underwear. It was like a visit to the doctor. He picked up the burlap, gave it to me, took a tub of axle grease from the closet and set it down between us. He said, "Go ahead," but I was so unimpressed I was barely erect. It was only as he rubbed the grease into the burlap that I became excited. There he was, in white silk, his fingers blackened with axle grease, playing in the folds of burlap. And, when I put my own hands into the tub of cool grease, nature took its course. I mean, I came.

It was this encounter that began my obsession with injuries, with the kind of deformities that weren't shown on film. From that night on, I sought out damaged goods.

There were all sorts of injuries, of course. Some of my lovers had lost fingers in accidents. Others were born with their defects. (One in particular was magnificent: she had only two fingers on her right hand. Her hand was only half its normal length, and the fingers seemed to sprout from the middle of her palm. Together, we rubbed linseed oil on a velvet dress; the most exquisite sex I've ever had.) Still others had damaged their hands with heavy weights or blunt instruments. There was something about the hopelessly unique that excited me, and after a while nothing else would do.

I gradually lost interest in the people around me and the films I was making. In the evening I would walk along Church Street or Jarvis appraising the outstretched hands, the minor injuries, admiring the way the prostitutes held themselves: bent forward in their robes, their hands level with my waist.

It was six months after all this that I had the first of my accidents:

I was on Church Street. It was mid-winter and dark, and the prostitutes were gorgeous, beneath the streetlights, in their colored robes.

A woman in a bright yellow caftan, her face veiled, put out her right hand.

"Company?" she said.

Her hand was beautiful. It was almost precisely maimed. Of her fingers there remained only stubs, pinched at the tips as though they had been cut with secaturs. Her thumb was undamaged, but it twitched like a frog's leg in electric current. I couldn't tell what kind of accident she'd had.

"Sure," I said.

We took a taxi along Dundas, passed the hotels in Chinatown, passed the places I was used to, but I didn't notice how far afield we'd gone. I was entranced. Her caftan was yellow as a sunflower and soft. Her hands smelled of vanilla. When we got out of the cab, I had no idea where we were though the neighborhood was no seedier than I expected.

We went into a narrow, grimy building. At the front desk was a young man who was bald, save for a circular patch of hair which drooped from the side of his head.

"Twenty for the room," he said. He barely looked up from the small television on the counter. When he had my money, he said, "Sixteen."

We went up the stairs, the woman and I. Bedsheets hung from the banister like laundry. The stairwell walls were splotched and stained, and lime-green where the paint had fallen off.

Number Sixteen was large, square, and white. A window, draped with lace curtains, was on one wall. There was no bathroom. A narrow bed stood in the center of the room, as though we were going to reproduce. I didn't notice the closet until a little later.

The woman pulled a tub of Vaseline and a large piece of burlap out from under the bed. The burlap had been used. It was gummy, black, and sucked as she unfolded it. It was so exciting watching her peel the cloth open, I pulled down my pants and underwear myself.

And then, as though the wind had taken it, the closet door banged against the wall. Someone said, "Hello, sailor . . ."

And the woman got up to wipe her hands on my coat.

"Pull up your pants," she said.

There were now two men in the room with us. One of them held a lead pipe by two fingers, as though it were a rat's tail. I was terrified, and it was like every other time I've been terrified: my head began to hum and all the colors in the room grew unbearably bright.

I reached down to pull up my pants. The man nearest me kicked my ribs and I fell over.

"That's the position," he said.

The other one sat on my arm.

"What's he worth?" he said.

I said, "Please, take whatever you want."

The woman had gone through my pockets and taken the money from my wallet, but she wasn't happy. She stepped on my hand. I cried out, and almost immediately the man with the lead pipe struck the side of my head.

From there I don't remember much. I stopped moving and fled to the places inside: my mother's voice calling me home, someone whispering, the sound of bedsheets as I slid out of them, my hands on a kitten's belly, stones in summer, the river at night . . .

When I woke, the hotel clerk was above me, gently slapping the side of my face.

"Some party," he said.

I was where they'd left me, my pants around my ankles, the blood on the side of my face like a second skin.

"It's time to go," said the clerk.

He helped me to my feet, but I could neither dress myself nor move my arms.

"You need help?" he said. "You want a taxi?"

I wanted a taxi, among other things, but there was no money, so I went down the stairs with my coat on my head, my pants held up by my arms.

2.

Carpals, metacarpals, phalanges: so many bones to break. My elbow had only been knocked out of joint, but my left hand was truly mangled.

During the months it took me to recover the use of my limb, I reflected on what had happened to me. What I couldn't understand was *why* it had happened. Had I sinned? Had I earned the woman's enmity? Was it destiny?

I had been a young man with beautiful hands. I might have modeled. I might have found work in legitimate films. I might even have painted, but would any of these other lives have changed my fate? It was possible, wasn't it, that every direction held the germ of my downfall? Perhaps the woman and her accomplices had been born with my image as part of their collective memory. They had been God-driven, conscious only of His will, a three-person vengeance....

That's the kind of thing I thought about for months. In fact, I did way too much thinking. At first I blamed myself for what had happened, and then society, then my assailants, and then myself, and then God (in whom I did not quite believe). I was bitter that my looks had been spoiled, and then grateful, bitter, grateful, bitter, bitter, bitter. It took me six months to dredge up thousands of small questions, and then a few more to realize that I couldn't answer them alone.

My recuperation was frustrating and dull, and exhilarating. I mean, my life was reduced to basics. I did little. I could barely cook for myself. I couldn't dress properly. I stayed in bed. That was the dull part. The exhilaration came from anger. While my mind was at work on the metaphysical questions, my imagination spewed out pictures of violence. I saw myself assaulting my attackers with a wide variety of implements: a pool cue, a gun, a breadknife, an automobile, garden shears. Wherever I was, whatever I was thinking, visions of carnage would overtake me and my heart would race. After months of that, I was fairly excited by the idea of vengeance.

Not that I was vengeance-driven. It wasn't so simple. I wanted to speak to the woman and her accomplices, to make them understand. I mean, I was civilized: I wanted dialogue. Still, I bought a gun and a permit and went back to Church and Carleton.

Six months had passed since my accident. I was now wiry and cheddar-faced and I kept my arm close to my body, tucked in. On the street I tried to walk in a consistently different manner, limping at every step and throwing my right leg out in front of me. It was unlikely anyone would recognize me, but I wanted to be sure.

My recuperation had been dull, but the next few weeks were excruciating. Time stopped. I spent hours on Church and hours on Jarvis.

I wasn't looking for a woman in a yellow caftan. That would have been risky, there were so many yellow caftans about that year. Instead, I was looking for her hands. I inspected each and every hand presented to me. Here, the fingers were similar, but the thumb didn't shake. There, the thumb shook, but there were too many fingers. Night after night it was the same thing: limping patience.

And then, a woman's voice asked, "Company?" with just the right inflection. And put out a hand with the right number of stubs, pinched at the tips, with a thumb that quivered in that peculiar way.

All that I had been through, all of my emotions, flooded my imagination, and for a second I was utterly confused.

She was wearing a hooded white robe over her winter clothes. She didn't even bother to look up at me. She bent forward, with some difficulty, and proffered her gorgeous hand. You could see she hadn't lost any sleep over my misfortune, and I felt a sort of pity, as though what I was about to do were more cruel than what had been done to me.

I leaned forward to look at her face. She bent down further to avoid me. She held her hand up and went down as far as she could without falling. So it was that, with my head almost touching the pavement, I first saw her face.

It wasn't the most propitious angle. The shadows were a bit distracting and the blood had rushed to her face, but there was something, something in her long, brown hair, black eyebrows, thin nose and flared nostrils, her high cheekbones.

"Want company or what?" she said.

"No, thank you," I said, and straightened up slowly and limped off, making sure to casually inspect the hands of the other prostitutes along the way.

At the first corner, I turned west, then north on Yonge, east on Carleton, and south on Church, so that I was on my way back to her.

It wasn't as though I had a plan. I mean, I wanted to kill her, but there were details to consider. I could:

1. Shoot her on the spot, without giving her a dressing down.
That was unacceptable.

2. Give her a dressing down, and then shoot her.
That was awkward.

3. Accompany her to a hotel, dress her down, then shoot her.
The best option—though she might recognize me en route and jump from the car.

4. Dress her down, accompany her to the hotel, and shoot her.
Which would call for the kind of brutal persuasiveness I wasn't sure I possessed.

5. Shoot her non-fatally, accompany her to the hotel, and dress her down. Which introduced the novel idea of a non-fatal

shooting, and all the mechanical precision that implied.

6. Dress her down, shoot her, and then take her to the hotel. Out of the question, for technical reasons.

7. Shoot her, dress her down, and then take her to the hotel. Out of the question, for similar reasons . . .

Aside from all that, there were her accomplices to consider. Where were they? (I kept the gun in my right coat pocket. The bullets I kept in my left, for fear I might shoot myself. Would I have time to clean the lint from the bullets, put them in the chamber, and then squeeze off three precise shots? I didn't think so.) And then there was her face. It had been a mistake to look so closely.

So, I returned to her without any real plan of action. This time, however, I crossed to the opposite side of the street as soon as I had her in view. I was about a block away, by a maple tree, when I stopped to watch her.

As far as I could tell, she did nothing out of the ordinary. She stood patiently, talking to no one. Then, when a certain type of pedestrian approached, she would bend forward, present her hand and, if there were no interest, return to her place on the pavement. Once or twice she looked up and her face was bathed in streetlight. Once, she looked in my direction, but without purpose, without interest. It was not one of her successful nights.

We had spoken to each other around midnight. At four in the morning, she took off her robe, put on gloves, and walked away. I myself was exhausted, having been approached by countless men and women looking for a good time, so I was happy to follow her.

She turned east on Queen, south on Ontario, east again, south again, then entered an apartment building just shy of Parliament. Not once had she bothered to turn around. She hadn't the slightest idea she was being followed, no idea that she might be followed. It was proof that she'd been sleeping the sleep of the Just. Had my bruised and broken body left the least impression on her soul? Was there a groat's worth of regret to be had from her? Did she have an inkling, even in her most private moments, that I might deserve vengeance? No, not at all, not a bit.

It was one of those winter nights when it makes no sense to be outdoors. There was an inch of wet snow on the ground. The moon was a platinum smudge, let's say, and the street was full of that peculiar light that makes everything appear vivid and two-dimensional. If I had been thinking straight, I would have gone home. Instead, I found an alley between two houses facing her apartment building. I walked up and down quietly, or sat in an empty garbage can from which I'd cleaned the snow.

This night, I was to have my most thrilling philosophical moment. Perhaps it was the cold. In any case, arse in a can, I seemed to glimpse a purpose to the universe: everything is pushed from behind or held in place. The stars couldn't move. The sun was held fast. The earth was constrained. All we could do, any of us, was spin. All that we want, and all we pursue, gives the illusion of movement, of liberty. There is no movement, no liberty, only local phenomena of such paltry significance it's a wonder we get out of bed for them.

It was quite a touching moment. I felt briefly at one with the stars. I might even have discovered deeper meaning to life, but it was cold. I jumped up and returned to thoughts of the woman and her accomplices, loading and unloading my gun in the dark.

At one o'clock the following afternoon, she stumbled out of the building. By that time I was cold, wet, and on the verge of hallucination. She was in a navy blue coat, a Peruvian hat, and white gloves, but I recognized her. I took up the chase.

And this was the longest, most confusing day of my life. I followed her in and out of fabric stores. She lingered in pharmacies. She sat for hours in a coffee shop, for minutes in a restaurant. She drank coffee. She ate fried eggs, boiled potatoes, dill pickles, and toast. I could not have predicted her activity if my life depended on it. (Of course, I'm not sure how much of this confusion was self-inflicted. My poor, frazzled brain saw only chaos. I can't tell if there was more to see.) The only thing I knew for certain was that she had no idea I was with her. I could have shot her any time.

That night I spent with Dante on the third terrace of purgatory, my thoughts at one with the course of the stars. I was clear as to the fate of several souls: mine, the woman's, and those of her accomplices.

"Company?" she asked as I approached.

"Sure," I said and felt almost holy as we stepped into a taxi and drove along Dundas, away from the safer places.

The "hotel" was the same. There was an older, gray-haired man at the front desk. He put out his hand, without looking up from the television on the counter. I paid him.

"Sixteen," he said.

It seemed to me the same sheets hung over the banister, and the walls were just as dirty. It was all very interesting. I was myself, but I was also an angel of death. She was doomed.

We went calmly into Number Sixteen. She approached the bed, bent down to pull out the grease and burlap I'd asked for, and it was then that I took the gun from my pocket, faced the closet, and fired four shots into it. (It wasn't easy, you know. I wasn't prepared for the recoil. Those four shots took a good fifteen seconds, but I managed to hit the closet where I wanted.)

There was a *clump*, like a body falling to the floor, but it didn't sound as if it came from the closet, not really. It sounded distant. The woman cried out in surprise, stood up, and moved away from me. I said, "Don't move."

But she kept moving towards the window. I fired at her feet, to get her attention. Then, I took four lint-covered bullets from my coat pocket. One of them fell to the floor, but I managed to put the others in their chambers. That fallen bullet was a giveaway: you could see I was upset.

Outside, there was a great deal of confusion: heavy footsteps and rushing about. It reminded me of a time when I had broken an expensive vase and my parents had come running.

"You remember me?" I said.

"No," she answered.

This wasn't at all what I'd expected. It was too diffuse. I was upset, but I wasn't really angry anymore, not at her. It seemed to me as though God himself didn't care if the woman or her partners lived or died.

"Take off your clothes," I said.

"You're not going to fuck me, are you?" she asked.

I looked into her eyes and saw nothing of interest. She wasn't there.

"Shut up and keep them on then," I said. But she went on undressing, prepared for the worst, though the thought of reproductive contact hadn't crossed my mind. I'd merely wanted to keep her busy while I dressed her down.

She stood naked before me, her left arm up to cover her small breasts, her right hand over her pubis, her thin body bent forward, her face looking up at mine. It was repulsive. If she'd said anything, anything at all, I'm sure I'd have shot her, just to get it over with.

The problem was I couldn't decide what to do. I didn't know *how* to dress her down. I had too many things to say but my mind was stuck on, "Do something. Do something." So, when I shot her in the leg it really was an accident. The gun went off. She cried out in misery and fell to the floor.

I won't pretend that any of this made sense to me, that I felt relief, that all the tesserae of my life suddenly formed a precise image. That didn't happen. I was as confused then as I am now. It occurred to me that she would get splinters if she lay on the floor too long, and then I walked out.

I left the hotel undisturbed, a police car passing by me as I hailed a cab. I don't remember what I was thinking, but it can't have been much.

3.

The moment I fired into the closet, all of Nature turned away from me. The spirit went out of the things around me. (I can't describe it any other way: the spirit of things receded, like the tide going out.) I was like a stranger to the world: the floor would take my steps, but no more; the walls supported my weight, but unwillingly; lights would illuminate and hinges turn, but despite me, not for me. I could have put my hand in a flame without having it burn, or breathed underwater without drowning. The rules no longer applied to me, though instead of feeling liberated I longed for the old order. I wanted to drown.

To put it plainly: my soul no longer recognizes its home. For two years, it has followed one path, while my body has followed another.

I wish I had the words to explain what I've been through, but there's so much I don't understand and still more I don't want to face. I could explain it all as Fate, I suppose, but that's not right. I could speak of "accidents," but that's not it either. What I need is a common language for body and soul, a language to articulate these lost years. I don't hold out much hope for it.

Still, all of this has been sinking back into the mire for some time now. I think of her much less often. I have nightmares of her face no more than once a month. Gradually, the world is coming back.

(This morning, for instance, I burned my toast and the smell almost brought me to life.) I've been building a bridge between now and then, without knowing.

I first became aware of this bridge while filming *Broken Knuckles*. I was rehearsing a scene with Irene Buttress. Our fingers looked beautiful as we rubbed freshly tanned leather. The little finger on her right hand was bent to a 45-degree angle, and I suddenly remembered how much pleasure her hands had given me, how pure it was to be in contact with a rough fabric.

That was a few months ago.

These days, I try to keep my right hand before the camera. (My left does have a certain *je ne sais quoi*, but I can't stand to have it filmed.) I earn a living, but I'll never go back to Church Street to admire the fingers.

It's the price I pay.

you don't see it, do you?, 1994. Wall text installation at
Thread Waxing Space, N.Y.C.
p. 247

Black Forest Wall, 1992. Wood, 144 x 332 in. Installation at
Documenta IX, Kassel, Germany.
pp. 249 (detail with viewer) and 256

The Triangle, 1994. MDF board, latex rubber, stainless steel,
iron, and glass, 33 x 76¾ x 59 in.
pp. 250 and 251 (interior detail)

Untitled (elephant footstools, elephant skull), 1988. Plastic-laminated wood
shelves, elephant skull, hollowed elephant feet, and zebra hide,
44 x 128 x 23 in. and 89 x 43 x 42 in.
pp. 252 and 253

Untitled (ironing board, exercise bike), 1995. Wood ramp, plastic and metal exercise
bike, metal ironing board with polyester cover, and plastic
and metal household iron, 60 x 150 x 239 in.
pp. 254–255 (detail)

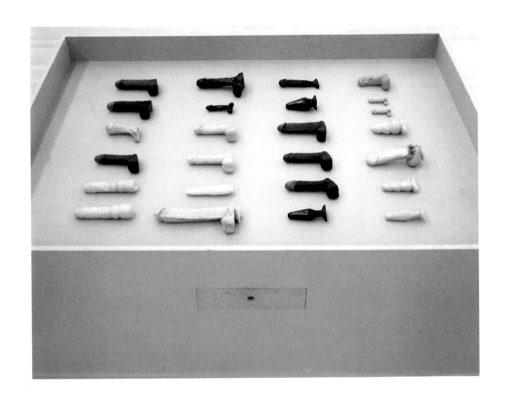

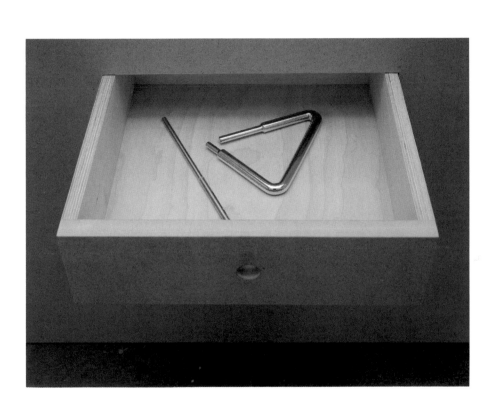

For most of his career, Haim Steinbach has charted the vicissitudes of objects between the borders of high and low culture. Assembling various consumer goods—from Nike shoes to Lava Lamps—on a series of triangular Formica shelves, his work in the 1980s related objects through variations of color, texture, and form, blending a strict, abstract Formalism with the psychology of advertising and display. These works conflated Marcel Duchamp's *Readymades* with the Minimalist "boxes" of the sculptor Donald Judd, but went farther than both in their representation of mass production and its impact on twentieth-century art. By buying the objects he used instead of simply finding them, Steinbach himself embodied the role of consumer. He also called attention to the gallery's role as a place of purchase, and made it a setting for the upward mobility of objects.

Steinbach's work was thus bound to the larger economy in a way that the more insular works of Duchamp or Judd were not. In this, he shared affinities with his more flamboyant contemporary, Jeff Koons, and also faced some of the same limitations in the early 1990s. Being so connected to the sphere of popular culture, both artists felt pressure to adjust their work as the larger climate changed. Steinbach, characteristically, returned to his sources.

His earlier emphasis on commodity, for example, had meant that the slyly enigmatic nature of Duchamp's *Readymades* was largely absent in his work, as was Judd's obdurate approach to abstraction. As if to remedy both of these lapses, Steinbach's recent works include drawers which slide from stark steel or Formica boxlike reliefs. In them, he places such nondescript items as a handful of dimes or a single embroidered handkerchief. A recent exhibition placed two labor-intensive devices (an ironing board and an exercise bicycle) on top of a wooden ramp, and surrounded them with framed images from Eadweard Muybridge's nineteenth-century motion studies and Michael Snow's more recent deconstructions of filmic narrative. Other installations featuring rusticated walls, each with trap doors that open into compartments or onto adjacent gallery space, evoke the voyeurism of Duchamp's *Étant Donnés*. In each instance, Steinbach has found his new focus in the discourse of implied connection, opening and closing, knowing and not knowing.

—Howard Halle

Composing Stick

The way of experience proper is the front door. Through the back, I carry my mother's body down into sleep. My mother lode. Ingrained vocabulary. The word abode of checkered origin. I dreamed I was human, but not sure it was possible. I refer to the factor of actuality, there being ambivalence. Charlemagne signed with a cross, which he inserted into the loops of the signature prepared by one of his scribes.

Any form of thought a spasm of pleasure if we could get at it. Mother cleared my throat. My mother tongue. Where do you put your hands when constructing a hypothesis? Or inner stairwell? The brain must be able to communicate every item of information received in one part to all its other paroxysms. Sleep at a distance. Or following a fish. A sense of unease may afflict the traveler, but the scribe must retain a steady hand.

The tide of dreams washes up in the sink. Too many chairs, even at midday. Mother succumbed to the antique love seat. My mother of vinegar. And potatoes. If there is physical interference between these and the so-called silent areas, things are seen but not recognized. The tarot showed La Papesse, La Mort, La Tour Abolie. We may say that compulsion is beveled blindness. Initially, printing seemed more an extension of handwriting than characters moving toward a plot.

Often our discoveries come as lucky accidents. A ring around the moon, a sign of pain. Mother in a different constellation of confidential. My mother of pearl. On moonless nights surrounded by sobs. The mechanism for opening the eyes more nearly tuned. Attention prowls among privacies. Furniture, pen, ink. A flicker of worry, dilapidated in its implications.

The exaggerated application of the principle of mere neighborhood. But many people can think better with eyes closed. The back of habit. Motherproof? House of cards. The projection of unconscious hostility greatly speeded up by the introduction of paper. After a pause, I practiced idleness. Fingernails pointed like banjo picks. Down endless corridors, up winding staircases, the slow and laborious process of writing.

The elements of consciousness such as the glass reflects. Doors open doors closed. Curtains, their capacity for surface. Feeling as big as the room, a child will dress up in her mother's clothes. My mother hood. Surely there are photographs to put in its place? An eyelid in the mind? When Gutenberg could not repay his debt, the banker Johann Fust confiscated all his material and hired it back to him. The hostility is cried down by an increase of tenderness, smoke blown into the room, or too sick for arrest.

CONTRIBUTORS

André Alexis was born in Trinidad in 1957 and moved to Ottawa in 1960. His plays have been performed in Toronto and Vancouver, and his work has been heard on CBC Radio. His short-story collection, *Despair and Other Stories of Ottawa*, in which a version of *The Third Terrace* first appeared, was published in 1995 by Coach House Press.

Hilton Als is a contributing editor to *Grand Street*.

Simon Armitage was born in 1963 and lives in the north of England. He is poetry editor at Chatto & Windus, and presents *Stanza*, BBC Radio 4's contemporary poetry program. He has written poetry extensively for television and radio, and his fourth collection, *The Dead Sea Poems*, will be published in the fall of 1995 by Faber and Faber. In 1994, he received a Lannan Award for his poetry.

Morton Bartlett was born in Chicago, Illinois in 1909. He died in Boston, Massachusetts in 1992. (Please see p. 176 for further biographical information.)

Georges Bataille (1897–1962) was a novelist, philosopher, and critic whose work has had a major influence on twentieth-century French literature and philosophy. The books published during his lifetime include *Les Larmes d'Eros*, *L'Expérience intérieure*, *La Part maudite*, and *L'Erotisme*. The translation of *Madame Edwarda* published here is excerpted from *My Mother, Madame Edwarda, The Dead Man*, translated by Austryn Wainhouse (Marion Boyars).

Samuel Beckett was born in Foxrock, near Dublin, in 1906. He moved to Paris in 1914 and lived there until his death in 1989. In 1969, he was awarded the Nobel Prize for Literature for his play *Waiting for Godot*. His novels include *Murphy* and the trilogy *Molloy*, *Malone Dies*, and *The Unnameable*. His plays include *Endgame* and *Happy Days*.

Michael Brodsky was born in New York City in 1948. He is the author of eight works of fiction (most recently "***" published by Four Walls Eight Windows) and a number of plays. He received the PEN Ernest Hemingway Citation.

CONTRIBUTORS

Alexander Cockburn is a syndicated columnist who contributes regularly to *The Nation*, *The Anderson Valley Advertiser*, *The Los Angeles Times*, and other newspapers. He has just published *The Golden Age Is In Us: Journeys and Encounters, 1987–1994* (Verso).

Guy Davenport is a poet, translator and essayist whose publications include *Tatlin!*, *Da Vinci's Bicycle*, *Eclogues*, *Apples and Pears*, and *A Table of Green Fields*. He received the Fiction Award from the American Academy and was named a MacArthur Fellow in 1991. He lives in Lexington, Kentucky.

Anne Doran was born in Calgary, Alberta in 1957. She has exhibited her work in New York at the 303 Gallery and the New Museum of Contemporary Art, and in Europe at the Stedelijk Museum, Amsterdam, and the Centre Georges Pompidou and Galerie Rizzo in Paris.

Walker Evans was born in St. Louis, Missouri in 1903. His work, which redefined the course of American photography, has been exhibited at countless museums, including the Museum of Modern Art in New York in 1933 and 1938, and was honored in a retrospective at the Art Institute of Chicago in 1948. He died in 1975. The photographs published here are taken from the collection of Harry H. Lunn Jr., New York.

Bob Flanagan, a Los Angeles writer and performer, is the author of several books of poetry and prose, including *The Wedding of Everything*, *Slave Sonnets*, and *Fuck Journal*. Selections from his current work-in-progress, *The Book of Medicine*, have appeared in numerous journals and anthologies, including *High Risk* (Dutton/Plume) and *Best American Erotica 1993*. He has appeared on stage with the Groundlings comedy improv ensemble, and in several films and videos. *Visiting Hours* made its East coast debut at New York's New Museum of Contemporary Art in September 1994.

Arthur Goldhammer is a writer and translator living in Boston. He has translated more than sixty works from the French. His translation of Maurice Lever's *Sade: A Biography*, published in 1993 by Farrar, Straus & Giroux, was awarded the American Literary Translators Association Outstanding Translation Prize.

CONTRIBUTORS

Hervé Guibert was born in France in 1955 and died of AIDS in 1991. Formerly a journalist for *Le Monde*, he was one of France's best-selling writers during his lifetime, as well as an acclaimed photographer. Guibert's work published in English includes *The Gangsters, My Parents, To the Friend Who Did Not Save My Life* (Serpent's Tail), and *The Man in the Red Hat* (Quartet).

Herondas's mime works were discovered by a scout from the British Museum in 1890, when he purchased a papyrus scroll from a group of Coptic tomb robbers in Egypt. Almost nothing is known about the author—neither his native city (Kos or Alexandria, perhaps), nor when he lived (the evidence points to the third century B.C.).

Mohammad Nurul Huda is one of Bangladesh's leading poets, the author of more than a dozen books of poetry, several volumes of essays, and a prize-winning novel. He is director of a division of the Bangla Academy in Dhaka, an institute for the study and publication of Bengali literature and folklore.

Yayoi Kusama is an artist and novelist who resides in Tokyo. Born in Matsumoto City in 1929, she left Japan in 1957 and spent the following fifteen years living and working in New York and Europe. Her works are included in the collections of the Museum of Modern Art, New York, the Whitney Museum of American Art, the Stedelijk Museum, Amsterdam, and the Centre Georges Pompidou, Paris, as well as in several major museums in Japan. In 1989, a retrospective of her work was held at the Center for International Contemporary Arts, New York, and in 1993, she was Japan's sole representative at the Japanese pavilion of the Venice Biennale. Her work was also included in the recent exhibition *Japanese Art After 1945: Scream Against the Sky* at the Guggenheim Museum SoHo.

Okura Kyojin is a poet and sculptor living in Hiroshima. He studied in Madison, Wisconsin in the 1980s.

James Laughlin's most recent book, *Phantoms*, with abstract photographs by Virginia Schendler, was published by Aperture in May 1995.

CONTRIBUTORS

Man Ray was born in Philadelphia in 1890. He studied at the National Academy of Design in New York and collaborated on several projects with Marcel Duchamp, before moving to Paris in 1921, where he became allied with the surrealist movement. His work was included in the *International Surrealist Exhibition* (1936) at the New Burlington Gallery, London, and in the *Exposition Internationale du Surréalisme* (1938) at the Galerie des Beaux-Arts in Paris. In 1968, he participated in *Dada, Surrealism and Their Heritage* and *The Machine as seen at the End of the Mechanical Age*, both at the Museum of Modern Art, New York. He died in Paris in 1976. The line drawings that are published here were first collected in *Les Mains libres: Dessins de Man Ray* (Paris: Gallimard, 1947).

Jann Matlock is Associate Professor of French Studies in the Romance Languages and Literatures Department at Harvard University. She is the author of *Scenes of Seduction: Prostitution, Hysteria, and Reading Difference in Nineteenth-Century France* (Columbia University Press) and the coeditor, with Marjorie Garber and Rebecca L. Walkowitz, of *Media Spectacles* (Routledge). She is currently completing a book on theories of vision, aesthetics, and the female body in nineteenth-century France.

Colum McCann was born in Dublin, Ireland in 1965. His first novel, *Songdogs*, will be published by Metropolitan Books in the fall of 1995. He has lived in Ireland, North America, and Japan and currently lives in New York City.

Christopher Middleton was born in Cornwall, England in 1926. He has lived in Austin, Texas, where he teaches German and Comparative Literature, since 1966. His collections of poetry and translations include *Selected Writings, The Balcony Tree, Andalusian Poems,* and *Floating Miniatures. Intimate Chronicles* will be published by Sheep Meadow Press in 1996.

John Montague is the author of *About Love* (Sheep Meadow), *The Figure in the Cave and Other Essays* (Syracuse University Press), and *The Rough Field* (Wake Forest), among other books. His *Collected Poems* will be published in the fall of 1995 by Wake Forest Press.

CONTRIBUTORS

Tosa Motokiyu was born in Hiroshima, Japan in 1955. He studied musical composition in Milwaukee and Madison, Wisconsin in the early 1980s. Since 1984, he has lived alternately in Japan and Sebastapol, California, where he has been engaged in translating and editing the manuscripts of Araki Yasusada.

Alexandra Munroe is a writer and independent curator based in New York and Tokyo. She organized the exhibition *Yayoi Kusama: A Retrospective*, held at the Center for International Contemporary Arts, New York in 1989 and her exhibition *Japanese Art After 1945: Scream Against the Sky* opened its U.S. tour at the Guggenheim Museum SoHo in the fall of 1994. The show will be on view at the San Francisco Museum of Modern Art with the Center for the Arts at Yerba Buena Gardens through the summer of 1995.

Taslima Nasrin was born in Mymensingh, Bangladesh in 1962. She completed a degree at the Mymensingh Medical College in 1984 and was posted as physician and medical officer in various Dhaka hospitals. She emerged in the late 1980s as a poet, columnist, and fiercely independent feminist, renowned for her bold public criticisms of Bengali society and the Islamic religion. In 1989, she began to write columns—commenting on social and gender issues such as *purdah*, prostitution, domestic violence, and female sexual oppression—for a Dhaka news magazine edited by her second husband. In 1992, a selected collection of these pieces was awarded the prestigious Ananda Prize, West Bengal's highest literary honor. In 1993, Nasrin's novel *Laija (Shame)*, depicting a Bangladeshi Hindu family which suffers atrocities at the hands of Bangladeshi Muslim extremists, was banned by the Bangladesh government. In September 1993, a fundamentalist Muslim leader in northeastern Bangladesh put a price on her head. Nasrin was forced to resign her government medical job and to petition the Bangladesh government for protection. In 1994, after Nasrin had criticized the *Koran* in an interview with *The Calcutta Statesman*, the Bangladesh government itself issued a warrant for her arrest. Nasrin went into hiding and Western governments began to intercede on her behalf. In August 1994, Nasrin was granted bail and flew to Stockholm, where she went into voluntary exile, and remains as a guest of the Swedish PEN writers' organization.

CONTRIBUTORS

Helmut Newton was born in Berlin in 1920 and is an Australian citizen. At sixteen, he began an apprenticeship with the Berlin fashion photographer Yva. He served in the Australian army from 1940 to 1944 and settled in Paris in 1957. During the 1960s and '70s, his photographs appeared regularly in numerous magazines in the U.S. and Europe. He is now a regular contributor to *Vogue* and *The New Yorker*. He has lived in Monte Carlo since 1981.

Geoff Nicholson was born in Sheffield, England and lives in London. He is the author of eight novels, including *Hunters and Gatherers* and *Everything and More*. His most recent novel, *Footsucker*, from which his story here is excerpted, will be published in the United Kingdom by Victor Gollancz in the fall of 1995.

Ojiu Norinaga is a doctoral student in Comparative Literature. He currently lives in Tokyo, where he teaches English for the Nippon School of Business.

Christopher Reid is the poetry editor at Faber and Faber in London.

Robin Robertson is from the northeast coast of Scotland. His work has appeared in *The London Review of Books, The London Observer, The Times Literary Supplement, The New Yorker,* and *The Yale Review,* among other publications.

Sheree Rose's videos, photographs, and slide presentations, which graphically explore the S/M subculture and the world of body modifications, have been shown at Cal Arts, LACE, the Rosamund Felsen Gallery, EZTV, the Los Angeles Gay and Lesbian Film Festival, the Center of Contemporary Art, Seattle, the Feature Gallery, New York, Southern Exposure, San Francisco, and The Kitchen, New York. Her photographs have appeared in numerous publications, including *RE/search #12, frieze, Art in America,* and the 1993 *RE/search* book *Bob Flanagan: Supermasochist.*

Aura Rosenberg has exhibited her photographs and sculpture throughout the United States and Europe. Recent exhibitions include those at the Neue Galerie in Graz, Austria, the Kunstlerhaus Bethanien, Berlin, the Centre Georges Pompidou, Paris, Terrain Gallery, San Francisco, and White Columns, New York. She lives and works in New York.

CONTRIBUTORS

Barney Rosset founded Grove Press and has been the publisher of Blue Moon Books since 1987.

Ralph Rugoff lives in Los Angeles and writes about art and visual culture. In September 1995, a collection of his articles will be published by Verso, and in the summer of 1995, the Museum of Jurassic Technology will issue his monograph on the Armenian microminiaturist Hagop Sandaljian. His notes on Bob Flanagan are adapted from a review that appeared in *ArtForum* in December 1993.

David Searcy lives in Dallas, Texas, where he continues to work on his second novel, *Last Things*, whose opening chapter is published here. Chapters from his first novel, *Ordinary Horror*, appeared in *Grand Street 44*.

Farida Sarkar was born in Rajshahi, Bangladesh in 1957. She has worked as a lecturer at Notre Dame College, as a free-lance journalist for Dhaka newspapers, and as an announcer for Radio Bangladesh. She is currently working at the Voice of America/Bangla Service in Washington, DC. Two volumes of her poetry have been published in Bangladesh.

Haim Steinbach was born in Rechovot, Israel in 1944. His solo exhibitions include those at the Guggenheim Museum, New York, CAPC Musée d'Art Contemporain, Bordeaux, and the Palais des Beaux-Arts, Brussels, among others. Group exhibitions include Documenta IX, Kassel, *A Forest of Signs* at the Museum of Contemporary Art, Los Angeles, *The Ninth Biennale of Sydney* at the Art Gallery of New South Wales, and *Les Courtiers du Désir* at the Centre Georges Pompidou, Paris. Steinbach lives and works in New York, where he is represented by Sonnabend Gallery and Jay Gorney Modern Art.

William T. Vollmann is a novelist and a journalist and a contributing editor and writer for *Spin* magazine. He lives and works in Sacramento, California.

Austryn Wainhouse is the owner of Marlboro Press, which publishes primarily literature in translation.

CONTRIBUTORS

Rosmarie Waldrop's most recent books of poems are *A Key Into the Language of America* (New Directions) and *Lawn of Excluded Middle* (Tender Buttons Press). Station Hill has published her novels *The Hanky of Pippin's Daughter* and *A Form/ of Taking/ It All.*

John Waters lives in Baltimore, Maryland, where he is writing the script for his new movie.

Carolyne Wright spent three years in Dhaka, Bangladesh on a Fulbright Senior Research Grant, collecting and translating the work of twentieth-century Bengali women poets and writers. She met Taslima Nasrin in 1990, and her translations of Nasrin's work have since appeared in *The New Yorker, Triquarterly, The London Review of Books,* and *Index on Censorship.* A volume of Wright's translations, *The Game in Reverse: Poems by Taslima Nasrin*, will be published by George Braziller in 1995.

Araki Yasusada lived in Japan from 1907–1972. *Joyous Young Pines*, a limited-edition selection of Yasusada's haiku, is available from Juniper Press. His notebooks are currently being prepared for book publication by Tosa Motokiyu, Okura Kyojin, and Ojiu Norinaga. (Please see p. 24 for further biographical information.)

Brian Young is a 1995 N.E.A. Fellow in poetry. His poems have appeared in *The Colorado Review, Chicago Review,* and *Another Chicago Magazine.* He is currently teaching English at a Korean university.

In *Grand Street 52*, Carol Volk's name was inadvertently dropped. She translated *The Game of Love and Chance*, a conversation between Paul Virilio and Jérôme Sans.

ILLUSTRATIONS

front cover Yayoi Kusama, *Dressing Table*, 1990. Mixed media, 72 in. high. Collection of the Sogetsu Art Museum, Tokyo. Courtesy of the artist and Fuji Television Gallery, Tokyo. Photograph by Norihiro Ueno.

back cover Aura Rosenberg, *Women Opposite Santis, Switzerland*, 1993. C-Print, 20 x 16 in. Courtesy of the artist.

title page Helmut Newton, *Untitled* (detail), 1992. Courtesy of the artist.

pp. 10, 14 and 20 Photographs courtesy of Photofest. **p. 10** Divine meets the Infant of Prague in *Multiple Maniacs*; **p. 14** John Waters with the cast of *Desperate Living*; **p. 20** John Waters and Divine, San Francisco, 1970.

pp. 33–40 Yayoi Kusama, *Fortress of Shooting Stars*. Five mixed-media works and three documentary photographs (title, date, and dimensions appear with illustration). Courtesy of the artist and Fuji Television Gallery, Tokyo.

p. 33 Photograph by Hal Reiff.

pp. 34, 37 and 39 Photographs by Norihiro Ueno.

p. 35 *My Flower Bed*. Collection of Centre Georges Pompidou, Paris.

pp. 36 and 38 Photograph by Shigeo Anzai.

pp. 36–37 Collection of The Hara Museum, Tokyo.

pp. 67–72 Bob Flanagan in collaboration with Sheree Rose, *Visiting Hours*, 1994. Mixed-media installation, total dimensions variable (title, media, and date of individual works appear on **p. 73**). Courtesy of the artist. Photographs courtesy of The Santa Monica Museum of Art, Santa Monica, California. **p. 67 and p. 72** Courtesy of The New Museum of Contemporary Art, New York.

pp. 117–122 Walker Evans, *The African Negro Art Exhibition, Museum of Modern Art, 1935*. Six untitled silver gelatin prints, 8 x 10 in. each (a list of the objects depicted appears on **p. 116**). Courtesy of Harry H. Lunn, Jr.

pp. 137–144 Aura Rosenberg, *The Dialectical Porn Rock*. Eight C-Prints (titles and dates appear on **p. 136**). **p. 137** 16 x 20 in. **pp. 138–144** 20 x 16 in. Courtesy of the artist.

pp. 156, 168 and 169 André Adolph Eugène Disderi, *Portraits of Berthier*, c. 1861. *Cartes de visite* printed from collodion glass negative. Courtesy of Harry H. Lunn, Jr. **p. 160 (left)** Gavarin Theatre scenes from *Le Charivari*, May 28, 1839; **(right)** Edouard de Beaumont, *Les Vésuviennes*, 1848. Lithograph. Courtesy of Jann Matlock and the Yale University Art Museum.

pp. 175–180 Morton Bartlett, eleven black-and-white photographs of crafted figures with wigs and custom-made clothing, c. 1940–60. Photographs 4 x 5 in. each. Courtesy of Marion Harris.

pp. 175 and 176 (left) *Reading Girl*, 28 in. high.

p. 176 (center) *Waving Girl*, 30 in. high. and **(right)** *Cheerleader*, 32 in. high.

p. 177 *Crying Girl*, 26 in. high.

p. 178 (top left) *Ballerina*, 28 in. high. **(top right and bottom left)** *Bathing Suit Girl*, 32 in. high, background painting top right by Morton Bartlett. **(bottom right)** *Boy on Beach (Self Portrait)*, 28 in. high.

ILLUSTRATIONS

p. 179 *Sitting Boy (Self Portrait)*, 28 in. high.

p. 180 *Girl at Beach*, 31 in. high. Background photo by Morton Bartlett.

pp. 193–200 Helmut Newton, eight untitled photographs, 8 x 10 in. each. Courtesy of the artist. **p. 193** 1992; **p. 194** 1988; **p. 195** 1993; **p. 196** 1993; **p. 197** 1995; **p. 198** 1981; **p. 199** 1995; and **p. 200** 1994.

pp. 208 and 212 JoAnn Wypijewski, five untitled photographs, 8 x 10 in. each. Courtesy of Alexander Cockburn.

pp. 221–228 Man Ray, four drawings and four silver gelatin prints (titles and dates appear on **p. 220**). Copyright © 1995 Artist Rights Society, New York/The Man Ray Trust, Paris/ADAGP. **pp. 221, 222, 224 and 226** Ink on paper, also courtesy of Editions Gallimard, Paris and Timothy Baum. **p. 223, 225 and 228** Also courtesy of Sotheby's, New York and London. **p. 223** 4 ¼ x 2 ¾ in. **p. 225** 3 ⅛ x 4 ¼ in. **p. 227** Also courtesy of Timothy Baum. **p. 228** 2 x 2 in.

pp. 247 and 249–256 Haim Steinbach, *you don't see it, do you?*. Six sculptures (titles, dates, media, and dimensions appear on **p. 248**). Courtesy of the artist and Sonnabend Gallery and Jay Gorney Modern Art, New York. Photographs by Beth Phillips (**p. 247**); Dirk Pauwels (**pp. 249 and 256**); Jorg Burger (**pp. 250–51**); David Lubarsky (**pp. 252–53**); and Oren Slor (**pp. 254–55**).

p. 270 Posted in lower Manhattan, April 1995.

You've just Won it all

Statement of Ownership

Statement of Ownership, Management, and Circulation (Act of August 12, 1970: Section 3685. Title 39. United States Code). No. 1. Title of Publication: Grand Street. No. 2. Date of filing: 1-19-95. No. 3. Frequency of issue: Quarterly. No. 4. Location of the known office of publication: 131 Varick Street, Room 906, New York, NY 10013. No. 5. Location of the headquarters or general business offices of the publisher: 131 Varick Street, Room 906, New York, NY 10013. No. 6. Name and address of publisher and editor: Jean Stein, 131 Varick Street, Room 906, New York, NY 10013. No. 7. Owner: New York Foundation for the Arts, 155 Avenue of the Americas, New York, NY 10013-1507. No. 8. Known bondholders, mortgages, or other securities: None. No. 9. For optional completion by publishers mailing at regular rates. No. 10. Extent and nature of circulation: Average number of copies each issue during preceding twelve months. No. A. Total number of copies printed: 7,000. No. B. Paid circulation: 1. Sales through dealers and carriers, street vendors, and counter sales: 3,200. 2. Mail subscriptions: 900. No. C. Total paid circulation: 4,100. No. D. Free distribution by mail, carrier, or other means: 950. No. E. Total distribution: 5,050. No. F. Copies not distributed: 1. Office use, left over, unaccounted, spoiled after printing: 1,650. 2. Returned from news agents: 300. No. G. Total: 7,000. Actual number of copies of single issue published nearest to filing date. No. A. Total number of copies printed: 7,000. No. B. Paid circulation: 1. Sales through dealers and carriers, street vendors, and counter sales: 3,980. 2. Mail subscriptions: 1,000. No. C. Total paid circulation: 4,980. No. D. Free distribution by mail, carrier, or other means: 1050. No. E. Total distribution: 6,080. No. F. Copies not distributed: 1. Office use, left over, unaccounted, spoiled after printing: 608. 2. Returned from news agents: 312. No. G. Total: 7,000. No. 11. I certify that the statements made by me above are correct and complete. Signature of editor, publisher, business manager or owner: Jean Stein, editor and publisher.

P.N.Review

'the most important current journal concerned with poetry'

'*Poetry Nation Review* both honours and belies its proud name. It is, today, the most incisive voice of a vision of poetry and the arts as central to national life--a vision with a vividly British quality. But it is also an international meeting-place, a denial of parochialism as are things deep-rooted.'
GEORGE STEINER

'The most important current journal concerned with poetry, *P.N.Review* is gaining its proper recognition, surrounding its admirably intellectual criticism with an even richer spread of actual poems.'
MARILYN BUTLER *Times Literary Supplement*

For more than two decades *PN Review* has been the British journal of significant poetic record, in which new and established poets -- in English from around the world, and in translation -- have found unusual hospitality, and the challenge of rediscovery, appraisal and reappraisal has been a constant vocation.

P.N.Review is available on subscription.

SUBSCRIPTION ORDER FORM

Name:_____ Address:_____

_____ Zipcode:_____

I wish to subscribe to *P.N.Review* at the yearly rate of $49.00. Please charge my Access (Eurocard)/ Visa account (delete as applicable)
Number: _____Expiry:_____

Name as on card:_____Signature:_____

Return this coupon to
P.N.Review 208 Corn Exchange Manchester M4 8BA
fax 061 832 0084.

SHENANDOAH

THE WASHINGTON AND LEE UNIVERSITY REVIEW

SHENANDOAH
44/1 $3.50

WINTER 1994

Betty Adcock
Neal Bowers
Frederick Busch
Fred Chappell
Philip Dacey
Northrop Frye
Brendan Galvin
Donald Hall
Seamus Heaney
William Hoffman
Andrew Hudgins
X. J. Kennedy
Nanci Kincaid

Kathy Mangan
William Matthews
Heather Ross Miller
Janet Peery
Gibbons Ruark
Lisa Sandlin
Robert B. Shaw
Cathy Song
Anne Tyler
Jeanne M. Walker
Robert Wrigley
Charles Wright

"...a magazine of exceptional beauty and power."
— *Small Press*

Prizes for Volume 44

| The Jeanne Charpiot Goodheart Prize for Fiction $1000 **Hodgson Van Wagoner** | The Thomas H. Carter Prize for the Essay $500 **Carol Ascher** | The James Boatwright III Prize for Poetry $500 **Debra Nystrom** |

SHENANDOAH
Troubadour Theater, 2nd Floor, Washington and Lee University, Lexington, VA 24450

Name _____

Address _____

City, State, Zip _____

Single issue: $3.50   Subscription: 1 year/$11

Grand Street would like to thank
the following for their generous support:

Cathy and Stephen Graham
Barbara Howard
Dominic Man-Kit Lam
The National Endowment for the Arts
Suzanne and Sanford J. Schlesinger
Betty and Stanley K. Sheinbaum

Back Issues of Grand Street

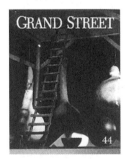

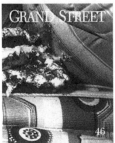
An Indispensable Collection

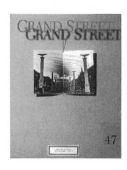

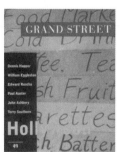
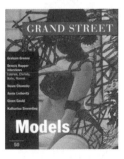

Now Available–Order While They Last

CALL 1-800-807-6548 or send name, address, issue number(s), and quantity.
American Express, Mastercard, and Visa accepted; please send credit card number and
expiration date. Back issues are $15.00 each ($18.00 overseas and Canada),
including postage and handling, payable in U.S. dollars.
Address orders to *Grand Street* Back Issues, 131 Varick Street, Suite 906, New York, NY 10013.

The bookstores where

GRAND STREET

can be found include:

Black Oak Books, Berkeley, CA
Bookstore Fiona, Carson, CA
University of California Books, Irvine, CA
Museum of Contemporary Art, Los Angeles, CA
Diesel Books, Oakland, CA
Logos, Santa Cruz, CA
Arcana, Santa Monica, CA
Small World Books, Venice, CA
Stone Lion Books, Fort Collins, CO
Yale Co-op, New Haven, CT
University of Connecticut Bookstore, Storrs, CT
Bookworks, Washington, DC
Oxford Bookstore, Atlanta, GA
Iowa Book & Supply, Iowa City, IA
Prairie Lights, Iowa City, IA
University Books, Iowa City, IA
Seminary Co-op, Chicago, IL
Von's Book Shop, West Lafayette, IN
Carmichael's, Louisville, KY
Waterstone's Books, Boston, MA
M.I.T. Press Bookstore, Cambridge, MA
Nantucket Books, Nantucket, MA
Broadside Books, Northampton, MA
Provincetown Books, Provincetown, MA
Books Etc., Portland, ME
Book Beat, Oak Park, MI
Baxter's Books, Minneapolis, MN
Walker Art Center Books, Minneapolis, MN

Hungry Mind Bookstore, St. Paul, MN
Whistler's, Kansas City, MO
Left Bank Books, St. Louis, MO
Nebraska Bookstore, Lincoln, NE
Dartmouth Books, Hanover, NH
Micawber Books, Princeton, NJ
Salt of the Earth, Albuquerque, NM
Collected Works, Santa Fe, NM
Community Books, Brooklyn, NY
Talking Leaves, Buffalo, NY
Book Revue, Huntington, NY
The Bookery, Ithaca, NY
Doubleday Books, New York, NY
Gotham Book Mart, New York, NY
St. Mark's Bookstore, New York, NY
Wendell's Books, New York, NY
UC Bookstore, Cincinnati, OH
Books & Co., Dayton, OH
Looking Glass Books, Portland, OR
Farley's Bookshop, New Hope, PA
Bradd Alan Books, Philadelphia, PA
Joseph Fox Books, Philadelphia, PA
College Hill, Providence, RI
Chapter Two Books, Charleston, SC
Open Book, Greenville, SC
Xanadu Bookstore, Memphis, TN
DiverseBooks, Houston, TX
Sam Weller's, Salt Lake City, UT
Williams Corner, Charlottesville, VA
Studio Art Shop, Charlottesville, VA
Northshire Books, Manchester, VT
Woodland Patter, Milwaukee, WI